PRAISE FOR *BUILDING B2B RELATIONSHIPS*

Relationships shape how we prioritize our time in life, and they largely drive how successful we are in life. In the professional services world, everyone will say they invest solid time in building trusted relationships. A little like everyone is client-focused. The reality is often quite different. I firmly believe that a lead indicator of the future success of any professional can be found in the quality of their relationship maps – both inside and outside of their organizations. I challenge anyone in our industry not to find at least one actionable insight from Ryan's book. I found several. He is the right guy to be writing this book.
Paul English, CEO, CLA Global

In the complex world of the global logistics industry, operational excellence is built on strong relationships across all levels, cultures, and time zones. This book provides actionable insights and a clear process for enhancing the relationships that matter most. It's an essential read for anyone responsible for driving performance in large-scale complex operations.
Trevor Hoyle, former SVP Ground Operations, FedEx Europe

This book brilliantly captures the essence of what it takes to build, maintain and effectively leverage business relationships. The insights and strategies provide a practical toolkit that any leader can apply immediately to drive meaningful results.
Mohit Joshi, CEO, Tech Mahindra

Dr O'Sullivan masterfully delves into the art of relationship-building, offering insightful strategies for sellers to forge authentic connections that drive successful outcomes. You can tell he's not only an expert on managing relationships, but he has lived it. This book is packed with actionable advice and compelling case studies, making it an indispensable guide for anyone aiming to thrive in B2B sales.
Timothy Kieth, CEO, Propense.ai

Ryan's book is a fantastic resource for anyone looking to gain a deeper understanding about the approach to building stronger B2B relationships. His experience and thoughtful approach shine through on every page, making complex ideas accessible and engaging. I've had the privilege of working alongside Ryan and have always admired his ability to approach challenges with clarity and creativity. This book is a reflection of his expertise and passion, and I have no doubt it will inspire and guide readers across all industries.
Rajesh Krishnamurthy, Group CEO, Expleo

Building B2B Relationships by Ryan O'Sullivan is a must-read for anyone serious about leveraging partnerships for business growth. Partnerships were the cornerstone of my success in scaling startups to $100 million exits, and this book is essentially a cheat code to partnership success. Ryan lays out practical, actionable strategies that make building and nurturing key relationships straightforward and effective. Whether you're a seasoned entrepreneur or just starting out, this book is an invaluable resource.
Callum Mckeefery, Founder, Reviews.io & Partner.io

Creating value across the private equity life cycle, from origination to portfolio management and exit, requires the ability to identify and develop trusted relationships with key executives. This book provides a clear framework with a pragmatic approach that any professional can use to strengthen relationships and achieve superior outcomes.
James Morris, Private Equity Executive

Dr O'Sullivan provides an insightful and thorough resource to people who understand the value and hard work of developing and nurturing relationships. He presents a compelling case for investing in relationship maps. The book is a 'must keep close' for those who want to excel.
Bruce Parker, Chief Sales Officer, Deloitte Canada (retired)

O'Sullivan has captured a compelling combination of process, science and human behaviour to bring together a truly actionable blueprint for creating better relationships beyond merely a sales process. From relationship mapping to cross-selling and responding to RFPs, this is a comprehensive guide to creating a B2B strategy for any business looking to grow and expand. This is best practice and then some!
Kevin Smith, KPMG former Chairman in London, Head of Private Enterprise in EMA and Global Chair of Emerging Giants

Ryan O'Sullivan does an excellent job of exploring the intricacies of building relationships, providing valuable insights into how sellers can identify and establish genuine connections that lead to mutually beneficial outcomes. The book offers practical advice and real-world examples that make it an essential resource for anyone looking to excel in B2B sales.

V S Srividhya, Global Head – Sales Effectiveness & Enablement, Infosys

What Ryan has done with this brilliant and authoritative book is take a contemporary perspective of all the factors that help to develop new B2B relationships and nurture existing relationships. Combining his professional experience with his doctoral research we have in this book an extensive account of how to explore the science and art of relationship building. A must-read for those entering sales, for account managers and for sales leaders interested in territory management and account planning.

Dr Philip Squire, CEO, Consalia

In a world of increasing complexity good relationships really matter. *Building B2B Relationships* is a wonderfully pragmatic book, full of wisdom, techniques and templates providing the reader with everything they need to know about developing and leveraging collaborative relationships, existing and new, to be successful in B2B sales. It will be a valuable reference point for our students and anyone working in B2B sales.

Dr Louise Sutton, Academy Director, BSc Professional Practice in B2B Sales, MSc Professional Practice in Leading Sales Transformation

Building B2B Relationships

*How to identify, map and develop key
relationships to win more business*

Ryan O'Sullivan

KoganPage

Publisher's note

Every possible effort has been made to ensure that the information contained in this book is accurate at the time of going to press, and the publishers and authors cannot accept responsibility for any errors or omissions, however caused. No responsibility for loss or damage occasioned to any person acting, or refraining from action, as a result of the material in this publication can be accepted by the editor, the publisher or the author.

First published in Great Britain and the United States in 2025 by Kogan Page Limited

2nd Floor, 45 Gee Street
London
EC1V 3RS
United Kingdom

8 W 38th Street, Suite 902
New York, NY 10018
USA

www.koganpage.com

Kogan Page books are printed on paper from sustainable forests.

ISBNs

Hardback   978 1 3986 1544 1
Paperback 978 1 3986 1541 0
Ebook   978 1 3986 1542 7

British Library Cataloguing-in-Publication Data

A CIP record for this book is available from the British Library.

Library of Congress Control Number

2024039742

Typeset by Integra Software Services, Pondicherry
Print production managed by Jellyfish
Printed and bound by CPI Group (UK) Ltd, Croydon, CR0 4YY

When we choose to devote time to a huge personal endeavour, like writing a book or researching for a doctorate, it means there is less time available for those closest to us. So I dedicate this book to my beloved and irreplaceable wife, Elisabeth, who had to fill the gaps in our family life during this period, and to my precious daughter, Charlotte, who missed having this time with her papa.

CONTENTS

6   **How to build and execute a relationship map:
     Step 3, relationship engagement strategy** 102

PART THREE
Putting the relationship-mapping process into action

7   **Relationship maps applied to key deals** 129

LIST OF FIGURES

ABOUT THE AUTHOR

Dr Ryan O'Sullivan is a senior executive, board member, business adviser, startup investor and university guest lecturer. He has spent his career perfecting and then evangelizing a 'relationship first' approach to growing revenue. This has resulted in many awards and accolades over his career, including the most net-new clients in a year on multiple occasions, fastest net-new client in the organization's history, first strategic deal (total contract value over $50 million) in a new country and largest deal in the organization's history. He has won deal of the year and salesperson of the year on multiple occasions and has been the number one annual revenue earner many times, often for consecutive years.

Ryan started his career generating net-new business and realized early on that focusing on prospect organizations where there was an existing relationship resulted in disproportionate success. Understanding the value of existing relationships led him to the following question: what are the contributing factors that determine a good-quality business-to-business relationship? Ryan was so determined to get a well-evidenced answer to this question that he spent seven years researching it, resulting in a PhD. He applied this evolved thinking to great success during his eight years at Infosys – a global IT services firm – and, more recently, where he has found his philosophical home, at relationship intelligence and mapping company, Introhive, where he has worked since early 2020.

He is a regular speaker on the subject of relationship mapping. Ryan is invited to present at corporate and industry events and guest lectures at various universities around the world, evangelizing how mapping relationships will increase your strategic deal wins and make key account management more effective. He also brings this insight to the boardroom, where for a small number of startup companies that have a particular focus on B2B relationships, he is involved as an investor, adviser or board member.

He currently lives in the South of France near Nice with his wife and daughter, where he enjoys long walks along the beautiful coastal pathways and around the many medieval villages, sometimes stopping along the way for a nice glass of rosé.

FOREWORD

I have been fortunate to have spent the past 30+ years collaborating with some of the most prestigious and innovative companies in the world, helping them to deliver value to their end clients. During that time there has been one constant: in every deal, in every project and in every account, it is the relationship that matters. They are important in good times, but when things go awry it is the quality of your relationships and good, open and transparent communication that will get you through.

When we think about the process of selling, it is really about your prospect or client taking a 'leap of faith' with you. The average salesperson is focused on 'convincing' them to take a leap into the abyss, and with the client's sense of trepidation and anxiety this can be hard for them. The best salespeople give clients the confidence to willingly walk the path suggested and with you by their side. That is because of the relationship you have forged which means they completely trust you and your organization.

This is the reason relationships are so critical – now more than ever – and we all inherently know this. We see that our client engagements are becoming more complex and competitive, with new technologies and a wider ecosystem of players. We also see that there are many more people involved in the decision-making process. So, those people and organizations that have complete visibility into who is involved and can effectively navigate their way through will have disproportionate success. This is what will separate the very best from the average, and with the advent of artificial intelligence it is my opinion that being average will not suffice in today's world.

I have had the benefit of working directly with Dr O'Sullivan and have witnessed firsthand how the process he has developed, and which he outlines in this book, has helped bring clarity and structure to an otherwise complex world. This has resulted in benefit for him, our organization and our clients. Whether you are an experienced businessperson or just starting your career, understanding the process of identifying, mapping and cultivating key relationships is a vital success factor. Dr O'Sullivan has literally written the book on how to do it, and it's a must-read for all businesspeople.

Lee Blakemore
CEO, Introhive

ACKNOWLEDGEMENTS

If I were to look back at my journey, I could probably tell a story of a carefully orchestrated and well-thought-out strategy that took me from my hometown of Leicester in the UK, to studying and working in many places around the world, to finally settling in the South of France. I could explain that each decision was part of a strategic plan to get me to where I am today. However, the reality of life is very different, and my path is defined by a small number of what I would call chance encounters, each of which shaped who and where I am today.

I'll save you from a full chronological timeline from my birth in 1978 and skip ahead to when I joined Infosys in 2011, an opportunity that came to me out of the blue through some work experience in my past. Throughout my career I have been very fortunate to have had great managers; none more so than my first manager at Infosys, Mohamed Anis. We immediately clicked when we met as part of the interview process, and then worked side by side – often late into the night – when I joined. I learned so much from him and from being part of the Infosys machine, in particular about how to actually be a consultant to your client and how to think big. This time also instilled a strong work ethic in my approach to corporate life – which has since proved to be a significant differentiator for me. One of the beauties of being at a large corporation is that you have the chance to work with so many intelligent and experienced people, and that was certainly the case with Matt Studholme. He personified the consultative selling approach, and personally working alongside him and seeing the rapport and respect he was able to build with such ease was truly an enlightening experience. Another person who had a profound impact on me and my path, both on a personal and professional level, was Ponsi Sundaram. He was a beacon of light, a real mentor to me and someone I often think about; may he rest in peace.

The final person I will mention from my time at Infosys is Mark Holden. It was during this time that my systematic approach to sales was further honed and crafted. His detail-oriented and methodical style was something that I embraced, and it took me to the next level. It was Mark who also supported and encouraged my decision to take on the part-time doctorate, which provided the foundational thinking for this book.

There were many times during my doctorate when I looked up to the sky and wondered why I had agreed to take this project on, alongside my full-time job and also considering that my wife had just given birth to our daughter. It turned out to be such a fulfilling experience; the immediate value was actually learning more about myself personally than enriching my professional life, but it has since opened the door to many wonderful opportunities, not least this book. I sincerely thank Dr Lillian Clark for making the effort to engage with me and then supporting my application process as well as her and Dr Beth Rogers for being part of my initial supervisory team. Dr Yuksel Ekinci and Dr Sianne Gordon-Wilson picked up from them and took me through the vast majority of the process, joined by Dr Phill McGowan towards the end to get me across the finish line. My doctorate delved deep into what defines a good-quality business-to-business relationship, and while it is generally accepted that leveraging relationships will result in better outcomes, it was after the doctorate that I started to realize where the gap actually lies. It is in the mapping of relationships at deal, project and account level. If you don't know who you know, and you don't know who you don't know, how can you be successful?

Then a chance encounter at an event led me to discover Introhive. I vividly remember seeing the tagline on their booth; it read 'In Business Relationships Matter' and I thought, 'exactly!'. They initially considered me a lead as I was working at Infosys, but through subsequent conversations with Adam Roberts and others it became apparent that there was an overlap between my doctorate, my business philosophy and their line of business, which is mapping relationships. So, the conversation quickly turned into something more and, quite frankly, I haven't looked back since joining Introhive. Considering that mapping relationships is Introhive's core business, there has been inspiration from too many people to mention; however, I have been particularly close to two people. I first heard the term 'servant leader' from Barry Glinski who epitomizes that sentiment, and when combined with his innate understanding of how to grow a business it makes for a perfect combination. He would often mention the idea of me writing a book, even before I had given it much thought, so thanks for planting the seed Barry and for all the encouragement. And if there has been one constant throughout my time at Introhive then that is Adam Draper. He is the consummate sales leader, which also includes a good mix of rolling his sleeves up and getting involved. He has always given me the right amount of guidance when needed and has been a staunch supporter of this book.

I was introduced to my book publisher, Kogan Page, via a social media post from Dr Grant Van Ulbrich. He had just published something with them and wrote about the experience on LinkedIn. So, this was the catalyst to explore the book idea further. He made the introduction, and it was a great pleasure to work through the book proposal process with commissioning editor Donna Goddard and have it accepted. The process from approval of the book to completion has been around 14 months, and Jeylan Ramis, as my development editor, has been fantastic every step of the way. Thank you to you both.

It was comforting to know that I had Ceri Daugherty by my side again; we worked together on my doctorate thesis, and she was a great sounding board and support throughout the whole process of writing this book. I would also like to make a special point of thanking a small number of people who stepped in towards the end of the process and gave me some critical feedback from the perspective of a subject matter expert. Although it caused me some heartburn to take all this on board in what was the final few weeks before my deadline, what they gave me truly raised the standard of the final output and for that I am very thankful. These people are Taiana Melo, Mark Berger and my original doctorate thesis supervisor, Dr Beth Rogers. Taiana picked up on a handful of words and phrases that were overused and became a distraction, and she suggested I sharpen the point in a few places. Mark reacted in the way I had hoped – with his bounding energy and enthusiasm – which led to numerous early morning calls and the sharing of handwritten sketches. The outcome was the three-step triangle you see as Figure 4.1, and a rewrite of how the three-step process is structured and presented. Beth's input was golden, and it was a privilege for me to benefit from her vast experience writing numerous business books over the years. She helped with a full end-to-end review to sense-check the ideas and the flow.

A final mention to the ten senior executives who were willing to share their knowledge and wisdom, each writing an introduction to a chapter. Thank you – your perspectives give extra credence to the content that follows.

A sincere thank you to everyone mentioned here within this acknowledgement page and, of course, there are so many more that aren't mentioned. Thank you to you all.

LIST OF ABBREVIATIONS

AI	artificial intelligence
BBC	British Broadcasting Corporation
B2B	business to business
CEO	Chief Executive Officer
CFO	Chief Financial Officer
CGO	Chief Growth Officer
CIO	Chief Information Officer
CMO	Chief Marketing Officer
COO	Chief Operating Officer
CRM	Client Relationship Management
CSM	Customer Success Manager
FOT	front office transformation
GBP	Great Britain Pound
HR	human resources
KAM	key account management
KPI	key performance indicator
ONA	organizational network analysis
RFI	request for information
RFP	request for proposal
ROI	return on investment

Introduction

It would be fair to say that you, the reader, do not need to be convinced that relationships matter, both in a personal and professional capacity. You can probably recount countless examples of when you've turned to someone you know for help, whether for advice on taking a new job, some insight into an organization or industry or for an introduction to someone you would like to meet. And the same is true on the other side, with people in your network coming to you for guidance, whether that be family, friends, coworkers, clients or others.

Instinctively, and anecdotally, we know that relationships matter and we value existing relationships differently from new ones. As explained by the global lead for sales effectiveness at one of the Big Four accounting firms, their own analysis shows why they win and it's because they have good relationships. They also know why they lose and it's not because of price or timing, but rather because they don't have good relationships. The data also wholeheartedly supports this, with a summary of Nielsen's[1] 2021 study reporting that 88 per cent of people trust a recommendation from someone they know. To add to that, in the book *Shift*,[2] Craig Elias states that from his analysis, when you are the first to engage with the key decision maker and with the right solution, you can win 74 per cent of the time. Bringing this all together, Heidi Gardner's research, as discussed in Gardner and Matviak's 2022 book *Smarter Collaboration*,[3] found that those who have more relationships generate four times the revenue compared to their peers with a smaller network.

I would argue that existing relationships are more important now than ever. This is because, on the one hand, it is now much easier to maintain existing relationships thanks to the shift to virtual meetings and with the various communication channels available to us. These include WhatsApp, LinkedIn and Facebook, and mean we can keep in touch even if that includes commenting on a post on LinkedIn or Facebook. However, alongside that, it is more difficult than ever to build new relationships through cold outreach. I say this as someone who started my career as a new-business salesperson. People are inundated with prospecting messages, whether it's automated outreach on LinkedIn or email cadences. This makes building new business relationships hard, and it's only going to get harder.

So, while there are many people out there today who can advise you on cold outreach strategies, this book takes a very different tack. It is focused on strategies to leverage your existing relationship network and will help to open your peripheral vision beyond what you might consider to be 'your network'. Just imagine how much more successful you could be if you could not only leverage your network more effectively but also the network of your coworkers. This book is anchored around helping you in three scenarios – winning key deals, delivering key projects and growing key accounts – and argues that instead of trying to build new relationships to grow your business, you should follow a 'relationship first' strategy. You will still be winning new business but will be winning it where you have the best chance of success, that is where an individual in your organization is connected to a decision maker in the prospective client.

In one form or another I have spent my career identifying, mapping and analysing stakeholder relationships. Included within this period is seven years researching this subject for my doctorate, and the past four years working for a relationship-mapping organization. Through that I have developed a tried-and-tested approach which has been honed by working on some very complex deals. These include a $100 million+ agreement which, in the later stages of the deal, required a group of people to be based in a hotel in a different country for a number of months. In this role my only job was identifying, mapping and developing the engagement strategy for key stakeholder relationships – just for that deal. While not every deal will be like this, there are certainly ones which have a comparative equivalence based on size and significance to your organization, and indeed to you on a personal level. So, it is to these key deals, the key projects that follow and the key accounts that you are managing that the three-step process I have developed should be applied – the ones that will move the needle for you.

- Step 1 is identifying and mapping the key stakeholders – if you don't know who the key people are, how can you influence them?
- Step 2 is conducting research and intelligence gathering on them – if you know who they are but don't know what is important to them, why will they give you their time?

- Step 3 is defining and executing on an engagement strategy – if you know who they are, and you know what is important to them, who is the best person to engage, through what channel and with what message?

The book is broken down into three parts. **Part 1** provides the foundation by explaining what trusted relationships are and why they matter, which is presented over the first three chapters. **Part 2** explains the three-step process, with a chapter devoted to explaining each step (Chapters 4, 5 and 6). Finally, **Part 3** comprises four chapters (Chapters 7, 8, 9 and 10). There is one chapter on implementing the process for each use case (key deals, key projects and key accounts), and the final chapter will help you put this into action. I have no doubt that if you master the relationship-mapping process and apply it in today's business landscape you will be on an upward trajectory, and this book will support you on that journey.

PART ONE

What are trusted relationships and why do they matter?

The next three chapters form Part 1 of this book, with each devoted to a different aspect:

- Chapter 1 makes the case for why relationships matter, both in our personal and professional lives.
- Chapter 2 explains in detail the definition of a trusted business-to-business (B2B) relationship.
- Chapter 3 introduces the concept of relationship mapping and describes its origins.

Part 1 provides you with some foundational knowledge to explain the hows and whys of relationship development. As you read these first three chapters, you'll notice there is a framework that provides a foundation for some of the things we simply take for granted. This is designed to help you understand how and why relationships work in the way that they do. Some of the main concepts and insights presented in Part 1 come from my doctorate research. Should you wish to explore the evidence underpinning this book in depth, my entire thesis is publicly available online and can be found by searching for 'Exploring business-to-business relationship quality in the IT services industry by Ryan O'Sullivan'.[4]

1

Why relationships matter

Introduction

GARY READER, KPMG – GLOBAL HEAD OF CLIENTS & MARKETS (RETIRED)
The significance of relationships cannot be overstated in both our personal and professional lives. In business, however, where transactions are not merely exchanges of goods and services but also of trust, understanding and mutual benefit, relationships serve as the glue that really holds everything together.

I spent a lot of my career looking after some of my organization's most important global relationships, and I recognized early on that for positive financial outcomes I had to do more than just ensure that a particular piece of work was delivered on time and to budget. I have lost count of the times I was asked in a meeting, 'So, what are you seeing in the broader marketplace?'. I had to be able to deliver insights and for my most important and strongest relationships, I made sure that I invested the time to be armed with those relevant insights. In a dynamic and rapidly evolving marketplace, staying attuned to emerging trends, challenges and innovations is paramount. The author mentions the importance of research and intelligence gathering, and to me this is key to any successful relationship-building activity and is key to ensuring businesses can tap into a wealth of knowledge and expertise. In turn it evidences commitment to both the relationship and the client's business more broadly and contributes to the building of the strong foundations necessary for long-term relationship building.

In my experience every successful business engagement will be underpinned by a network of robust relationships. Whether it's building alliances with suppliers, collaborating closely with partners or cultivating loyalty among clients, the ability to cultivate and nurture meaningful connections is absolutely key. In the competitive world of B2B interactions, where multiple organizations vie for attention and market share, building and sustaining relationships are not nice-to-haves, they are strategic imperatives.

For me, one of the most important reasons relationships matter in a B2B context is that they enable the building of trust. Trust forms the solid foundations of any enduring partnership, serving as the cornerstone upon which fruitful collaborations are built. In the world of business, which is filled with complexity and uncertainty, organizations will always be searching for partnerships that can help provide stability and reliability. Establishing trust helps to generate a sense of confidence in the buyers of services, and that their best interests will be at the heart of the supplier's thinking. Another important element worthy of mention is that strong, trusted relationships really help parties navigate any issues and challenges which inevitably arise.

The chapter talks about how what might start as transactional engagements can evolve into something much deeper and stronger. Strong relationships can help suppliers better understand the needs and preferences of their clients. This, in turn, can lead to suppliers better tailoring products to the needs of their clients, delivering better outcomes for clients and a potential expansion in the footprint of the supplier at a particular client. Probably, all of this is best summed up in what is an often overused but relevant phrase – strong relationships result in a 'win-win' for all parties.

I mentioned earlier the importance of trust when dealing with the inevitable difficulties that can emerge from time to time between suppliers and their clients. I would also contend that strong relationships can really help in times of adversity or economic downturn. Put another way, they can help provide an element of business resilience. Friends look after their friends and it has certainly been my experience that in challenging times, such as the financial crisis of 2008–2010, the clients in which I had invested many years building strong relationships with were the ones that would continue to look to work with me, if at all possible.

It is also relevant to point out that strong relationships can actually spark innovation and creativity in a way that something more transactional cannot. By bringing together the diverse perspectives and expertise of suppliers with their own people and other partners, businesses can potentially unlock new solutions and capitalize on untapped opportunities. In my experience such events can only take place if there are strong relationships, and thus strong trust between all the parties involved.

It is my view, based on many years of experience, that strong relationships lie at the heart of successful B2B interactions. In a world where there is access to so much data and information, it is becoming harder and harder for many suppliers to offer a truly unique, differentiated product. Relationships are by definition bespoke and personal (even though of course they are often built in a business context), and thus continue to present the supplier with the opportunity to offer something different from their competition. They enable the building of trust and ultimately a positive outcome for all parties involved. However, they should never be taken for granted and as this chapter and book set out so clearly, a lot of work must be put in to build and maintain them. The good news is that the author does set out some tried-and-trusted techniques to help in this critically important area.

The value of relationships

Introduction

Relationships come in all shapes and sizes. This book won't only open your mind to the power that will come to you by leveraging them, but will also help you to extend your line of sight beyond the obvious meaning of what an existing relationship might be. To achieve this, it evaluates relationships from two perspectives. First, an individual perspective of your own relationships and how they can help you to be more successful and, second, from an organizational perspective through leveraging the business relationships of everyone in your organization. However, since we are focusing on leveraging existing relationships let us briefly consider how those relationships may initially be built.

It all starts with the openness and curiosity to meet people and build relationships. It can be difficult to know what will come from every interaction, but I'm sure we've all had instances where we talk to the person next to us on the train or plane and it turns into something we didn't expect. I've had many of these. For example, in relation to a screenplay I wrote when I was a student, I was on a train and by chance ended up sitting next to a producer at the BBC. We got talking and one thing led to another and I found myself at BBC Head Office talking to the team responsible for *Silent Witness*, which at the time was a very popular TV series in the UK. We developed my screenplay into a TV show with eight episodes. Alas, there wasn't a happy ending to this story, but it almost certainly only went that far because of that chance encounter on the train, and my willingness to start a conversation.

So, whether in a personal or professional context – and often these can cross-pollinate – relationship building is the foundational element to success in life. It might not be a straight line to what you want, but it could be insight, guidance or other types of learning. Relationships can start anywhere, but it is how you develop them that matters in business relationships. There is a lot to be said for having a focus on something tangible; indeed, there is a school of thought that says when you are aligned to specific outcomes the universe will organize itself around your thoughts. Now I'm certainly not going to that extent, but I'd argue that when things are front of mind you do have a higher probability of connecting conversations to these things. So, it is simply about building relationships and, in the words of Louis Pasteur, is the case that 'Chance favours the prepared mind'.[5]

The three objectives of relationship building in business

When it comes to relationship building in a business context, we are broadly striving for one of the following three outcomes from an interaction with someone:

- First, to **gather research and intelligence** about something of significance to you.
- Second, to ask if a person can help with **an introduction to someone** they know.
- Third, to **engage directly with a decision maker** or someone relevant to you.

This is an iterative rather than linear process and while each can happen in isolation, and might lead to the next, there could be a scenario where all three of these happen in one interaction. For example, you meet a key decision maker on a deal you are working on, they give you some important intelligence into the scope, and they also provide an introduction to some other stakeholders. So, think about the people you meet in relation to the objectives you have in the context of these three potential outcomes. Let us look a little closer into each one.

Research and intelligence gathering

This first outcome is concerned with learning new insights that can help you. We've established that building relationships is a good thing and if you have some specific direction and motivation that is driving that conversation then things can happen. However, the foundational level of relationship building is research and intelligence gathering, and this will be discussed at length later in this book. Understanding the lie of the land is fundamental to everything that follows, and there are many directions research and intelligence gathering can take you. These are usually dependent on who you are talking to (their job level and openness to share), and such interactions provide great depth that will help you to define the right strategy and execution plan.

So, whoever you are engaging with always have your antenna on to pick up any **insights into the client's business,** industry, competitors and market trends. This will **provide a deeper understanding** of the client's current situation and future needs. By being informed you can position yourself with more credibility and be more effective in anticipating potential challenges and/or opportunities that the client may face.

Getting introductions

A second outcome from relationship building is getting an introduction, either directly to the people you would like to meet (e.g. the decision makers) or someone else who might be able to help with some research and intelligence gathering. Perhaps you have already experienced in your own day-to-day life that leveraging your network to tap into their network has a huge multiplier effect. While the advent of LinkedIn has been a game changer for this concept there is still a lot of room to further maximize its potential.

Introductions from existing relationships carry a higher level of credibility, and the trust they have for the individual giving the introduction is in some ways transferred to you. People are **more likely to meet you** when it comes from an introduction. If this approach is successful, you can usually bypass the gatekeepers preventing you making contact directly.

Meeting with the decision makers

Sitting at the pinnacle of the objectives of relationship building is the opportunity to meet directly with key decision makers, perhaps on a key deal, or a key project or a key account. Of course, if this type of opportunity materializes then you had better be prepared for a solid conversation and, hopefully, will have had time for adequate research and intelligence gathering.

FIGURE 1.1 The three reasons we have a meeting

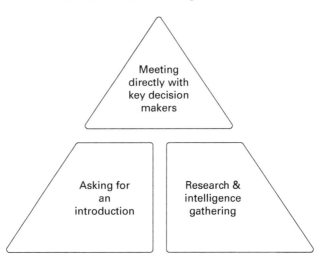

As we can all appreciate, relationships tend to be built on a one-to-one (individual) level, but there is also the B2B or organizational level to consider. The next sections set out the value from each of these two perspectives.

Individual level: Relationship capital and where to invest it

Think about any situation you are in, personally or professionally, and think about how a relationship with someone can help you to solve the problem or achieve the outcome. When we think about relationships in that context it's very hard to argue that they do not matter. Relationships can offer insight, provide advice and guidance and can give you introductions. In any facet of life, relationships are the fuel that gets you to where you want to go, from A to B; actually, **relationships can be a jet fuel** to get you there a lot quicker.

While the Covid-19 pandemic was an awful time for the world, some of the change it drove has been beneficial. For example, it led to an acceptance of relationship building via virtual media. As a result, **today, it is possible to build a relationship with anyone** wherever they happen to be in the world. When you think about this possibility it's incredibly powerful and is possible primarily because we are meeting on video calls. Prior to Covid-19 there were options such as joining by conference call if you were not there in person; however, I remember the star-shaped phones we had in our meeting rooms or the clunky officed-based video conference technology (which never seemed to work). So, in 2020, there was this step change to Zoom, Microsoft Teams and other such technology that enabled virtual meetings to be more spontaneous and easier to schedule. With the visual component, although they couldn't replace the 'watercooler chats' that are possible with in-person meetings, they do permit creation of some of the chemistry that only used to happen with in-person meetings. Now you can have these inter-actions, pretty much with anyone, any time, any place – but perhaps many people are now taking this opportunity for granted?

Relationship capital

With this step change came an abundance of opportunity when it comes to building and nurturing relationships. With such an abundance it begs the question of where you should invest your time and energy in this regard. To help you think about this, I'd like to introduce the concept of 'relationship capital', which can be used to evaluate your relationships. To do this you should consider your relationships as an asset, just like other asset classes. For example, think about all of your wealth across the different types of asset classes: equity in your house, your retirement savings and your other savings and investments. That is your financial capital and you can total it up to give you a number.

You can also think about your academic capital which is your schooling/ education, and the qualifications you may have. That is something you have been building and which is an asset of your own that you can carry around with you. You also have professional capital which includes your CV, and the history of your employment. All of these are assets and in this same context I'd like to suggest that you can consider relationship capital as the aggregate of all of your relationships, i.e. the totality of your personal and professional relationships. **Your relationships are an asset that you own** and that you build.

I challenge people to think about relationship capital in that context. It's an asset that can be leveraged for your own and others' benefit, and which can be brought to the table to solve a problem or utilized in a conversation about a new job or a new role.

Where to 'invest' your relationship capital

Now we've discussed the concept of relationship capital there comes the question about where you should 'invest' your relationship capital. The answer is the same as where we invest our financial resources, that is, where we believe we'll get the best return, and **when the return is working we continue to invest** in the same place. Think about the time and energy you invest into building and nurturing relationships in the same way. The 'return' you get does not necessarily mean what you personally 'get out' of the relationship. This is too much of a one-dimensional view as relationships are much more complicated than that. Instead, I'd categorize the return on investment (ROI) as 'one party getting value', which certainly does not mean only you personally getting value, but that one or more of the participants (one of whom could be you) is getting value. The ideal scenario is that both parties are getting value, but the point I want to make is from a sales perspective: when it is you knocking on their door, the person you are interacting with needs to get value for them to want to continue engaging with you.

An objective assessment of the return needs to be considered to determine if it's worthwhile, in particular when aligned to your personal and professional objectives. Our intuition and life experiences will tell us that existing relationships matter, and that leveraging an existing relationship will be more rewarding than dealing with someone with whom there is no relationship. The next section discusses some of the tangible outcomes.

THE THEORY OF HOW RELATIONSHIPS WORK

Taking all of this into consideration I would like to introduce you to a relationship theory that sits at the heart of all relationships and which explains how and why relationships form. It's called social exchange theory and states that to build a relationship with somebody you need to give them something of value. When you look at the historical significance of this theory it goes back thousands of years and is still practised today in many cultures. If we think about this in the modern business context, it's not physical gifts that we are bringing to people when we want to start a relationship but rather – in the business context – value. So, we really have to be bringing value to individuals to set the relationship off on the right trajectory.

This concept really defines what is at the heart of all relationships. Social exchange theory states that for any relationship to succeed there should be a fair return gained from the effort spent to maintain the relationship. Once this concept is understood it's possible to see it everywhere, whether in business relationships, friendships or romantic relationships.

All relationships need to begin somewhere, and that is usually with one person making the first move to interact with another. For example, in the case of building business relationships there could be an exchange of relevant information, providing insights on what one party wants or needs. From this fundamental basis a relationship can start. Social exchanges – as opposed to economic exchanges – are not able to be reduced to a single quantifiable exchange rate, but are an amalgamation of a variety of tangible and intangible exchanges.

Consider a romantic relationship where there may not be an explicit economic agreement in place; however, each side makes tangible and intangible contributions. Such tangible contributions could include financial support, use of a car or a place to live, while intangible contributions could be effort, love, inspiration, knowledge, empathy and companionship. However, the benefits that are received during any social exchange are not absolute and may be valued differently by different recipients. Nonetheless, the basic essence of social exchange theory can be reduced to the following simple formula:

$$\text{Profit} = \text{Benefits} - \text{Costs}[6]$$

Working backwards through the formula, costs are inputs such as spending money and your time or effort on a relationship; noting that a cost within a relationship could also be tolerating the negative aspects of a partner, such as things that are particularly annoying or unpleasant. Next, benefits are those positive elements received – both tangible and intangible. The outcome of the formula – profit – is the difference between the two. Using this, relationships where there is a positive balance of profit can be seen as positive while a negative balance denotes a negative relationship. The more negative a relationship is the less likely it will succeed. However, the calculation is personal and is internalized; thus, individual to each person.

It would therefore be expected that two individuals in the same relationship would have different calculations. In addition, the calculation is constantly being recalculated as the relationship continues. Thus, a deficit at one point might be offset based on previous or anticipated times of profit. However, there is an implied obligation to reciprocate at some level, albeit the timing and nature of the return may not be known at the time of exchange.

Organizational level: Why relationships are important

In the last section we discussed relationships at an individual level. This section explores relationships at a B2B (organizational) level. Business relationships can be categorized into one of three types: transactional, facilitative and integrative. There are other definitions using other terms, but these broadly capture the three categories.

- **Transactional relationships** can be considered as basic. These relationships are focused on the efficient conduct of small, routine, commoditized or one-off purchases. Typical examples are office supplies or cleaning materials. However, professional purchasers see advantages in automating as many categories of purchase as possible. In these relationships the supplier is undifferentiated from its competitors.

- **Facilitative relationships** involve the exchange and/or sharing of resources as part of a tactical solution. There is still little differentiation between the supplier's offerings; however, some efforts will have been made to work together to reduce the costs, risks and other factors related to maintaining the business relationship. An example would be a supermarket outsourcing storage and distribution activities to a logistics supplier.

- At the highest level are **integrative relationships**. These involve strategic thinking, including influencing each other's direction, where open, two-way dialogue exists as part of the joint pursuit of continued success. This is a collaborative relationship where the supplier and client solutions are designed to fit together to offer enhanced performance.

There is merit in and a place for all three types of business relationship. Indeed, it would not be possible for an organization to only invest in integrative relationships; a balanced portfolio of relationships is needed. However, rich and complex integrative relationships are the pinnacle that organizations strive to achieve. These are the 'trusted partnership' relationships and are **the focus of this book**. An organization's relationships are probably the most important asset they have, and while there are tools and mechanisms to value a brand, relationships tend to be an intangible asset. Nonetheless, it is difficult to measure their value, which can pose significant challenges.

If we consider the powershift from supplier to client, nowadays **the client is more sophisticated** and more demanding, with access to more information such as pricing, competitor data and product intelligence. This shift has been made possible largely due to the ease of access to information and, as a result, clients are now able to better educate themselves through desktop research and talking to peers and others (they do their own research and intelligence gathering!). This leads to them becoming more informed and knowledgeable and results in **clients being in a greater position of power**, thus making more effective purchasing decisions.

Consequently, as clients are becoming more informed the quality of the relationship becomes more important than ever. In fact, it could be argued that it's **the quality of your relationships that are now the differentiator** between you and your competitors. If we think about this in the key account context, an organization's largest and most important clients are getting bigger and more complex, as are the depth and breadth of its relationships.

Building trust at an organizational level

Trusting an organization is complicated, and the more trust an individual has the more comfortable they are sharing information. Of note is that the person on the client side must be comfortable with the supplier organization as a whole as well as the individual people they interact with. The added layer of complexity is that there are many people on the client side who need to have this comfort with many people on the supplier side, and all these people will have an opinion on whether they are comfortable with the supplier organization. Remember though that an organization does not have feelings. It is the combination of people in an organization and their shared values and business culture that generate trust.

A key part of the message of this book is to open your line of sight to **visualize all of the relationships** from your side and consider who they touch on the client side. In doing so, it can be helpful to consider that B2B relationships can be separated into two broad categories. First, relationships with existing and prospective clients; basically anyone you are trying to sell to. Second, relationships with the partner ecosystem including suppliers, outsourced functions, intermediaries and government agencies; essentially, any party not considered a client or a potential client.

Acknowledge that **your clients consider you to be a supplier to them**. Their perception of your purpose is that you help them to help their customers. So, in that spirit the purpose of a successful relationship is that over time the parties increase their cooperation, commit resources, absorb new knowledge and develop new methods which combine to create better business outcomes for all parties. So, organizational trust depends on both parties creating value for each other. The supplier's brand has to deliver on its promise, and the client's brand needs to do the same for its end customers. This relies on everyone collaborating and trusting one another.

Clients: Impact of high-quality relationships with suppliers

One of the most important impacts of a client having high-quality relationships with their suppliers is that it makes the solutions or products they offer for sale more reliable. This is achieved through collaboration, resulting in:

- Shorter product delivery cycles
- Lower costs
- Higher-quality output, and
- Increased reliability

It's the way suppliers behave with clients when the relationship quality is high that makes this material difference. If the relationship is good then suppliers are more likely to invest time, effort and resources into **ensuring the quality** of goods or services they provide is of the highest standard. Suppliers will also be more likely to **prioritize requests** over those of other businesses with whom they have weaker or less reliable relationships, and when the relationship is strong it often means that the supplier feels a higher level of personal accountability.

At the heart of putting this into action is communication. Higher-quality relationships often mean more **open and effective communication** which can help eliminate misunderstandings and misalignment of expectations. If things do go wrong a strong relationship allows for more open and honest feedback, making it easier to troubleshoot and resolve issues collaboratively. This openness is invaluable when it comes to continuous improvement.

On the product development side suppliers tend to be more **willing to adapt** their products or services to meet specific needs when there is a strong relationship. In such situations where there is a level of trust in place, suppliers are going to be more likely to suggest new ideas or innovations to businesses with whom they have strong relationships. This can potentially give them a **competitive edge**. In addition, it's commonplace for preferred clients to get first access to new offerings, allowing clients to have input into the product roadmap and to stay ahead of the competition.

What clients are really striving for is a competitive advantage, and when all of the things just described come together this is what it can create. So, when you have reliable, innovative and flexible suppliers willing to go the extra mile you can gain an edge over your competitors. This can manifest in many ways, from being the first to market with a new product to adapting quicker to market demands; thus, being able to offer better quality or more customized solutions. Greater profit can be gained through increasing the business and operational performance which then improves the market and financial performance, and the share price or value of the organization increases. The end result is **increased shareholder value**, which is the primary purpose of any for-profit organization.

Suppliers: Impact of high-quality relationships with clients

Having considered the impact of high-quality relationships on the client side, let us now consider the impact for the supplier. The outcome of delivering increased shareholder value to a client is **client satisfaction** and all other benefits that flow from this. The main benefit being that a satisfied client is likely to continue doing business with you. This creates **customer loyalty**, as once clients are satisfied they are likely to become loyal and stick with you over a longer term. This isn't just beneficial in terms of revenue, it's also positive for the supplier's brand since happy clients are more likely to share positive experiences within their network, leave positive reviews and otherwise endorse the supplier. This form of **word-of-mouth advertising** is not only free but arguably the most credible, and considering this type of endorsement comes from an existing relationship it's perfect to promote it within this book!

Loyalty leads to **customer retention**, which is much more cost-effective than acquiring new customers, thus, amongst other things, helping to stabilize revenue streams. As a result, revenue from an existing high-quality relationship usually has a more streamlined communication and support process where both parties understand each other. This familiarity should reduce misunderstandings and the need for reworking, leading to a **lower cost to service**; however, I wouldn't want to encourage complacency about communication here. It's just that when there are existing channels already established there should be more clarity on the route to take, but you still need to get it right. In addition, clients who already understand the supplier's value proposition and have experienced positive outcomes are going to make quicker buying decisions, leading to **shorter sales cycles**. This also requires **fewer resources** to be spent on marketing and sales efforts. However, it's important to note that large accounts often have high costs to serve compared to a smaller account, but obviously more revenue should be generated per person assigned to the account.

Good-quality relationships lead to **higher sales** as existing clients who have built a good relationship with a supplier are often more open to exploring additional products or services. They already trust the supplier, so the barrier to additional purchases is lower. This enables cross-selling and up-selling opportunities that might not be as readily available with new or less-engaged clients. In addition, clients with strong supplier relationships are more likely to allocate a larger proportion of their budget to that supplier rather than spreading their spending. This **greater share of a customer's spend** in a particular product/service category can be a competitive advantage, particularly in saturated markets where clients have many suppliers to choose from. It also provides a sense of financial security for the supplier, as a larger share of wallet usually means more predictable and substantial revenue streams. However, with this higher concentration of revenue in a smaller number of clients comes added risk, so awareness and acceptance of this risk is important, as is having appropriate guardrails and mitigation strategies.

The culmination of many of the previously mentioned benefits contributes to **increased profitability**. Then, perhaps counterintuitively, clients who perceive a high level of value in a good relationship often have a **propensity to pay more** for the same services or products. This willingness is usually because they see additional value in the reliability, quality and ease of doing business with the supplier. They may view any premium as a fair exchange for the reduced risk, enhanced service they receive or getting access to innovation; this is particularly valuable in competitive markets where price can erode profitability.

Indicators of high-quality relationships with clients

The most frequently observed indicators that your relationship with your client is going in the right direction are listed below.

- **Length of the relationship:** longevity in a business relationship is often an indicator of mutual benefit and satisfaction. A lengthy partnership suggests that the supplier is consistently meeting or exceeding expectations and delivering value to the client over time. It can also indicate a level of comfort and understanding that makes the working relationship more efficient and enjoyable for both parties.

- **Growing revenue from a particular client:** when a supplier sees consistent revenue growth from a specific client, it's generally a strong indication that the relationship is healthy and beneficial for both parties. Growing revenue signals that the client values the services or products being offered and can also be an indicator of customer satisfaction.

- **Expansion into different parts of the organization:** if a supplier starts by working within one sector of the client organization and then sees its portfolio expand to include other sectors, it is an excellent sign that things are going well. This indicates not only satisfaction but also trust since the client is willing to bring the supplier into different areas of their business.

- **Progression in the complexity of work:** when a supplier-client relationship matures to the point where more complex projects or tasks are assigned, it demonstrates a level of trust and confidence that can only be earned over time. It also offers the supplier an opportunity to showcase a broader range of skills and capabilities.

- **Awards or accolades for work with the client:** winning awards for work done in partnership with a client not only boosts the supplier's reputation but also reinforces the strength of the relationship. Such recognition usually comes from successful projects that required strong collaboration, innovation and execution.

- **Referrals from the client:** this pinnacle is achieved when a client is actively referring the supplier to other potential clients. It's clearly a sign they are happy with the outcomes they are receiving. Referrals come from a place of trust and indicate the client's satisfaction with the supplier's work. So, they are prepared to not only risk damaging their own reputation by recommending a particular supplier but in some ways are also trying to enhance their reputation by helping their peers to be more successful.

What we've learned in this chapter

We have learned six key things in this chapter:

- How relationships make a difference to our success.
- What we seek in B2B interactions.
- How to define organizational relationships and organizational trust.
- The value of good relationships with suppliers (for clients).
- The value of good relationships with clients (for suppliers).
- Indicators of good relationships.

What's coming next

This chapter explained why relationships are important. Chapter 2 is a summary of the findings from my doctoral dissertation and will explain what factors contribute to a high-quality B2B relationship, and how these types of relationships develop to become trusted.

2

What are trusted business relationships and the key steps to build them

Introduction

PHILIP GROSCH, PWC CANADA – RETIRED PARTNER
This chapter discusses in great detail what defines a relationship built on trust. Our focus as executives has always been to build trusted business relationships, and it is a central objective for all B2B organizations. This is because we know that moving from a transactional to a trusted relationship results in increased value creation for all parties involved.

Organizations that embraced this potential have made significant investments in client-facing executives and their supporting teams in the form of training and enablement as well as in technology. These efforts have resulted in stronger and more trusted relationships that B2B organizations can leverage to broaden and deepen their presence. Those organizations that recognize and harness this opportunity create a true competitive advantage. Just imagine if everyone at your organization could have access to and leverage the trusted relationships that exist across it, including those they were not aware of.

But while on paper these trusted relationships are enterprise 'assets', ironically, they are often closely held and difficult to get insight on. So, to put this into action requires the answers to three questions:

- How can we uncover 'who knows who and how well they know them'?
- How do we expose these powerful relationships at the time they are needed, e.g. to a pursuit team on a key deal trying to understand existing relationships across a set of key decision makers?

- How can we incentivize the 'relationship champions' to leverage their relationships to benefit the organization?

I have spent many years in the pursuit of answers to these questions and as you will read about in this book, better processes and technologies have come a long way in exposing answers to the first two. In addition, as the power of AI continues to accelerate, the accuracy and speed of doing this will only improve. But from my experience, the answer to the third point is arguably the more difficult one. This is how to motivate those individuals who have the trusted relationships to lean in and support their colleagues and the wider organization. The solution to this requires more in-depth thinking around compensation structures to incentivize collaboration and behavioural science-led change management efforts.

Dr O'Sullivan's book explains how you can get started on this journey and seize the enormous opportunity of leveraging the trusted relationships that already exist within your organization. It starts by understanding what a trusted relationship actually is, which is covered in this chapter, before going on to discuss the process of addressing those three very important questions.

My research

My doctoral journey started in September 2014 and lasted for seven years, but I had been curious about relationships for a long time before; specifically, how and why they formed. When you step back and think about what constitutes a high-quality B2B relationship, the specific components and the behaviours, it is not an easy question to answer. But let me ask you to think of one word that defines a high-quality B2B relationship – what is the first word that comes to mind?

This story may help you answer that question. The data generated by my research was a series of in-depth interviews with C-suite executives who worked at global companies, many of them Fortune 500 or Global 2000. I asked them a very simple question: 'Thinking back throughout your career, who was the best person you ever worked with from the supplier side? Someone that really made the difference.' Perhaps surprisingly they were all able to immediately think of someone (you could see a spark in their eyes when this person's face came into their mind). We then talked about what made that person so special. These conversations lasted around 45 minutes, so we were able to get into a lot of detail. When I transcribed all the interviews to prepare them for analysis, I created a word cloud of the most common words and phrases. Can you guess which five letter word was there, right in the middle in huge letters? It was TRUST.

We will read a lot within this book about aligning to the priorities of key stakeholders. When I asked the participants to think about the best person they had ever worked with, without exception everyone chose someone who was working on a top-priority project for them. For several of them this was a career-defining project. So, if you want a key stakeholder to think of you in this regard, you have to be working on things that are important to them.

This chapter will present the details of what behaviours contribute to building and maintaining trust. The first part is from an individual level (the relationship between two people), and the second part is from an organization-to-organization level (at a client and supplier level). For trust to form in B2B relationships both aspects need to be working in the right way.

My research aimed to identify experiences and opinions that my respondents had in common. So, the behaviours were experienced by the client at the same time, all of the time. From the rich insights generated by my research with decision makers, I was able to determine how best-in-class suppliers manage their client relationships.

How trust builds between individuals

The first interactions

Before someone will open up to you and start to trust you there is a stage called 'mutual disclosure' where each party is sizing the other up. At this stage they are deciding whether they want to invest time in the relationships and are trying to determine if this person can bring value to them. This is something that we can all relate to; we all know that you don't get a second chance to make a first impression. This phase in the trust-building journey is an extension of that common expression, and this 'sizing up' can take just a few seconds. Consider when you are meeting someone for the first time. Even subconsciously you draw some conclusions immediately based on how they are dressed and their body language.

The key to this phase is linked to what happens in that first 'meaningful' interaction. Ideally this would be a face-to-face meeting; however, it could be a virtual meeting or a phone call, but whatever the medium some key things need to happen very early on for them to consider you worthy of further investment of their time. For example, if it is you asking for a meeting with a senior executive, the balance of power will always be in their favour. Although you will know who they are, it's unlikely they have done much research on you. A lot hinges on this first interaction, so, from the client's perspective let's consider some important things during this first interaction.

- **Demonstrate knowledge:** my research identified that the number one thing you need to do as soon as possible is demonstrate you can bring them value. This often comes in the form of your knowledge and experience, such as in a particular subject, a domain, an industry or a technology. But, this has to be **linked to their priorities,** and the sooner you are able to do this the better. It helps position you as an equal, someone they can learn from, and a number of participants felt it was a **peer-to-peer conversation.** If you fail to do this then the relationship may drift into a pitch, or perhaps rest on small talk or discussing inconsequential items. It's unlikely the relationship will shift to a trusted partner status where they take immense business value from the interaction and will likely stay (at best) at the 'two people that enjoyed chatting to one another' level.

- **Not overtly 'selling':** perhaps unsurprisingly, one characteristic that was wholly negative and an immediate turn off was when the client felt that the person from the supplier was overtly selling to them. It was their opinion that the average salesperson was not willing or able to understand the client's needs and support them on a journey to better outcomes. One participant referred to the **average salesperson as lazy** and stated that they actively avoid interacting with such people.

- **Clash of personalities:** while having a shared sense of humour and outlook on life will certainly help relationships prosper, one thing that **spells disaster** is when there is a clash of personalities. There was a sense from participants that when there was a clash of personalities it was difficult to overcome. One recalled an experience where they had spoken to the head of the organization and told them that they would **take their**

business elsewhere if their account manager was not changed, all because of a clash of personalities. More is discussed later in this book about understanding your personality, determining someone else's personality type and then adapting your communication style to suit.

How to make the first interactions successful

Considering what we have just discussed about the importance and significance of the first interactions, there are three things you can do that will position you more favourably in front of senior executives and help on the trust-building journey. These are, first, coming to the meeting prepared; second, listening to what the client is saying; and, third, creating a compelling solution.

- **Coming to the meeting prepared:** the concept of coming prepared – that is having researched and understood the client context and **coming to the table with value** – was a big differentiator for clients. This links back to what we discussed in Chapter 1 around social exchange theory – as a sign of what the relationship means to you, you bring a gift. In the modern B2B context that gift is some form of value to them. So, to come prepared means **conducting proper research and intelligence gathering** prior to meeting with a key executive, as this will help you understand what is important to them. As you will come to understand, this is a **central theme in this book**. This point is fundamental to the relationship-building process. To accentuate this I am going to present three direct quotes from the C-suite executives I interviewed.

  A lot of other what I would call perhaps 'just salespeople' would come in for a meeting with me and they'd say 'so, where does it hurt, then?' I would, quite frankly, throw them out because if they're going to meet somebody who is running the technology function, **they had better have done their homework and if they haven't, they are sloppy,** and if they are sloppy the chances are the quality of their products is going to be sloppy.

  I think to understand: understand you, understand what your objectives are, understand the objectives of your company and what you're trying to deliver. If you don't understand the person, what makes them tick, **if you don't understand** the project that they're working on or the programmes they are working on, what the objectives of those programmes are, **then it's very difficult for them to offer services that are going to meet the needs.**

> What impressed me about him was **the diligence with which he researched and talked to a lot of my direct reports**, and a lot of other people in the business, before he came to me with some ideas about making things better, even before I had thought that perhaps I had a problem. So, here was an individual who **I was already beginning to trust** and I just felt was somebody who I would listen to.

These words so powerfully describe the impact of, on the one hand, doing thorough research and intelligence gathering and, on the other hand, the impact on their perception of you if you don't do it. Later in the book there is a whole chapter devoted to research and intelligence gathering, but essentially this is spending time to understand the priorities of the key stakeholders, their departments and the organization as a whole. This can be done by conducting desktop research and by talking to people who share insight and intelligence with you.

- **Listening properly:** the importance of listening cannot be underestimated, and the common mantra of 'we have two ears and one mouth' certainly holds true here. Moncrief and Marshall[7] go so far as to state that it is the key to any relationship, be it personal or professional. We know this from our own interactions with people; if you feel the other person is not listening to what you are saying and is distracted, then this becomes annoying. One participant stated that the thing the best person they had worked with did was listen carefully, and they spent time with them to really understand what was being said. They felt that was true engagement.

- **Creating a compelling solution:** the outcome of having the **knowledge base** and the experience that permits you to have a peer-to-peer conversation with a client, coupled with the right amount of **research to prepare** for the meeting and then **listening properly** will lead to creating a solution that will address the priorities of the key decision maker and wider organization. This will take the relationship to the next level. When this fails it will impact your business, and one participant recalled a conversation where they had made it clear to the supplier company that the salesperson they sent was not understanding what they (the client) wanted. Consequently, they would be unlikely to discuss any future requirements while that person was their contact.

Success! Trust is now forming, but what is the definition of trust?

There are three facets that combine to create trust: ability, integrity and benevolence. Each will be discussed below.

- **Ability**, credibility and effectiveness: all interview participants mentioned the importance of an individual's knowledge, which helped build their **credibility**. Their experience and knowhow are crucial contributing elements to their ability, but the second part to having ability is being **effective**. The participants want to work with people who make their lives easier and enable them to move forward in an efficient manner. Having people that can **'get on with it'** is seen as very appealing. Proving you can make things happen, both with your own organization and, crucially, within the client organization, is a huge contributing factor to having 'ability' and, thus, building trust.

- **Integrity**, honesty and reliability: there is a much-attributed quote, the message of which is that if you have integrity, nothing else matters, but if you don't have integrity, then nothing else matters. Thus, being open and honest is a prerequisite, as is talking about difficult subjects as they arise. When there is a level of **honesty** and a sharing of vulnerabilities this bene-fits everyone. According to participants, clients want that level of trans-parency – what a number called **'the unvarnished truth'**. One participant stated it perfectly when they said that a lack of honesty leads to a loss of trust. There is a fantastic book written on this subject called *The Trans-parency Sale* by Todd Caponi.[8] The second part is being **reliable** and **following through** with what you commit to do, and when someone fails on their commitments these failures obviously have an adverse effect on the relationship. A number of participants mentioned the cliché of the person 'over promising and underdelivering'. That is one thing, but it comes back to understanding the wider client context, with one partici-pant stating that the consequence of a supplier failing to do what they have said they will do can impact the wider client organization and can also impact upon the client's reputation. There was particular disdain for what the participants called **tardiness**, **lateness** and/or **lack of punctuality**. Essentially, they were unlikely to trust anyone who said they were going to be at a meeting at a certain time or said they were going to deliver something at a certain time, and then failed to do so.

- **Benevolence**, client orientation and intimacy: benevolence is having the intention to do a good job and genuinely caring about the client's interests. Participants mentioned that it was obvious to them when the individual from the supplier cared. They can tell from their expressions, by their senti-ment and their disappointment when things do not go right. Almost all participants mentioned the importance of a **professional conscience**, or what otherwise might be called **work ethic**. Indeed, a shared professional conscience, essentially, wanting to do a good job, being emotionally invested and having a good work ethic meant the most. For example, one participant referred to both sides taking pride in their work which created a position of mutual respect where both are striving for excellence. This is **client orientation**, the sense that you should always be thinking from the client's perspective. Putting yourself **in your clients' shoes** is a crucial mind-set when it comes to building trust. For example, clients don't care about a salesperson's targets or a sales quote. A number of participants said that the very best from the supplier side did not expose them to any type of pressure to achieve a particular sales quota or target; the client understood that there were targets, but it did not come across in a negative way. One participant felt that **nine out of ten people from the supplier side were focused on their targets**, so they felt that it was actually only one in ten that were focused on the business outcomes of the client and keeping their promises.

We have discussed the clear structure and process to building trust at an individual level. In those first interactions, demonstrate that you have knowledge to help them address a particular business problem, avoid overtly selling to them and avoid a clash of personalities. You can do this by conducting adequate research prior to the meeting, listening during the meeting and the output being a solution that addresses their priorities. With these things being done, trust will be forming. The specific characteristics of trust are demonstrating ability, integrity and benevolence. If we translate this over to an organizational level we see a similar structure and process.

A top tip to building trust with someone is to work on a deliverable together, whether that be a key executive presentation or other form of output. Through the process of jointly brainstorming and building it together, relationship capital is built. The more intense and high pressured the project, the closer the ties become – all participants had these types of interactions with the person they were describing from the supplier organization.

How to build trust between organizations

The first interactions

When building trust between two organizations, in the first interactions the supplier needs to demonstrate that they are a good fit. They have to give the client confidence that things will work out well. At the individual level it would be less likely that a client would have heard about you prior to meeting, notwithstanding them doing their own research prior to meeting. However, the client is more likely to have heard of the supplier organization – and perhaps even worked with them in the past. So, they may have some preconceived notions. But in the same way that there was a sort of dance between the two people at an individual level, when they were sizing each other up, a similar thing happens at an organizational level. My research identified three items that were important here.

- **Capability to deliver:** this is somewhat obvious but important nonetheless. The supplier the client is engaging with should be relevant to their business and the priorities that it wishes to address. As we will see in the next section, trust forms through tangible experience, but at this stage it's the supplier's job to convince the client that they have the right level of experience, knowledge, best practices and credentials in their field. Almost all participants focused on this element as being an important step with regard to them starting a business relationship. To achieve this level of comfort they look to a history of delivery in similar types of projects and, ideally, in a similar industry to theirs. Of note is that almost all participants had unpleasant experiences where they 'had been burnt in the past'. Collectively, this was something they were very careful about exposing themselves to, and there were differing reasons as to why this happened, from the supplier being too ambitious to what they considered to be the supplier being deliberately misleading.

- **Cultural fit:** in the context of my research this relates to how the two companies align based on cultural values, beliefs and practices. The analogy of a marriage was used by one participant, especially when it is a strategic relationship that affects the client's customers. In those scenarios it is crucial that the supplier has a similar culture to the client. One participant recounted a relationship with a supplier who wanted to understand how they worked and was interested in their culture and how they – the client – did business. This showed a remarkable level of emotional intelligence.

- **Partnership mentality:** expanding on this is recognizing the value of a closer, more cooperative style of relationship, and this has many benefits for both sides. As with any relationship, effort needs to be put in. There needs to be continual dialogue, understanding and comprehension of each other's businesses. Analysis of the research data revealed that a partnership mentality means being proactive, such as bringing in experts to give advice even when there is no revenue stream. It also involves approaching the relationship holistically, with the supplier considering themselves 'part of the team', making investments and 'putting skin in the game'; essentially, trusting each other to work in each other's best interest.

The components of trust at an organizational level

This next section summarizes the three core elements of trust that the supplier needs to deliver against in tangible terms. When the client experiences these things in a positive way then trust is forming.

- **Quality:** this is in two parts–quality of the people and quality of the outcome. Experienced clients can draw conclusions based on the **quality of people** they are presented with as to how successful the project is going to be. A number of participants gave specific examples of how the ability of the key person on the supplier side to either get the best people initially or replace people when they were not performing was fundamental to trust forming. This links back to being effective as part of trust at an individual level. Assuming the technical solution is fit for purpose, good-quality people lead to a **quality service,** which is the tangible outcome the clients buy. If it is consistently high then this leads to a perception of reliability and integrity, and the formation of trust. Ultimately, this leads to customer loyalty and a client's willingness to recommend. One participant referenced the 'bait and switch' tactic where the 'A-Team' are presented during the proposal stage but lower-quality personnel are used in the delivery of a service once the contract has been agreed.

- **Governance:** understanding how two organizations work together on a day-to-day basis is imperative. Some participants identified ineffective project governance as the single most likely reason relationships fail. Having a **good project management methodology,** breaking things down into manageable chunks of things that can be delivered, having very open discussions around status and about the services to be delivered as well as putting improvement plans in place with ownership and follow-up were all raised as important elements of successful project governance. Another dimension to this was being **flexible** and accommodating. With projects in flight and the pressure to deliver, clients demand more room within the relationships with their suppliers, for example, suppliers being willing to undertake work immediately on the assurance that a purchase order would be progressed as soon as possible.

- **Problem solving:** with all complex relationships there are inevitably problems that need to be resolved, and most participants mentioned the importance of the supplier **being transparent** when problems did arise. There was an understanding at an executive level that a small problem not addressed early on could create bigger problems down the line, perhaps outside of the supplier's purview. Reluctance to share problems at the earliest opportunity has a direct impact on levels of trust and, in the same spirit, being open and honest helps to build trust. While being transparent is paramount, most of the participants also said that the very best suppliers also stepped in to **take ownership** to solve a problem. A pattern emerges of the average supplier assuming it is the client's problem, and the client having to prove that it is the supplier's fault for them to consider doing anything about it. However, the best of the best suppliers handled it in a different way. As such, when a problem needs to be resolved, whether the contract is referenced or not, the client needs their support as part of a concerted effort to resolve the issue. The good suppliers come out directly with the problem statement and also produce different solutions and alternatives. One participant reflected on a particular supplier who ensured all the right people (regardless of seniority) focused on fixing the problem, maintained communication and got the problem solved. All this without first determining how much they would get paid for it.

Outcomes of delivering successful projects with a supplier

We discussed the benefits of strong client and supplier relationships in Chapter 1, and it might be no surprise that participants all agreed that the ultimate expectation of any supplier relationship is to deliver tangible business outcomes. However, when I delved deeper into what they got personally out of delivering business outcomes, they mentioned three things:

- **Personal satisfaction:** almost all participants stated that they got a sense of satisfaction from new knowledge and new experience, with one participant stating that being challenged and seeing how they could meet that challenge made them feel successful.
- **Career enhancement:** if individuals are not working on projects that inspire and motivate them this in turn affects their levels of job satisfaction. When the successes that they personally deliver arrive they then get

recognition and plaudits. Participants mentioned that a successful supplier relationship can have a positive impact on their career and personal reputation. For example, one participant referred to solving a particular problem as being a career enhancer, and that such an experience enhanced their relationship with the supplier involved.

- **Replicating success:** participants were asked, directly, if they moved roles would they be more willing to work with a supplier that had been successful for them in the past, and all agreed they would do this. They wanted to do this because they had experience working with this particular supplier, they knew each other and had been successful together in the past. One participant specifically mentioned assembling suppliers who they knew were effective across different contexts. However, there was acknowledgement that this approach is not necessarily fair on other suppliers.

To conclude, in those first interactions at an individual level when someone is trying to build trust, them being able to bring value to the key stakeholder is the key to starting a trusting relationship. To know what is valuable to the key stakeholder requires in-depth research and intelligence. This sits at the heart of everything. At an organizational level you also need to demonstrate that your organization can help by way of having the experience and credentials, and that the two organizations fit together well and will work in harmony. Then, when you execute as described, trust will form both at an individual and organizational level.

What we've learned in this chapter

We have learned five key things in this chapter:

- The important things when meeting someone for the first time.
- Research and intelligence gathering is a fundamental precursor to building trust.
- How individuals build trust.
- What organizations need to do to build trust.
- What the outcomes are of trusting relationships.

What's coming next

This chapter explained what factors contribute to trusted relationships. In Chapter 3 we bring this to life by zooming out and explaining the power of visualizing the relationships as they are connected to one another.

3

Introducing relationship mapping: What it is, its origins and why it is important

Introduction

ANDRAS VICSEK, MAVEN7 – ORGMAPPER (A LEADING ONA COMPANY) –
FOUNDER & CHAIRMAN OF THE BOARD

Understanding the web of relationships both within and outside your organization isn't just beneficial, it's essential. At its core, relationship mapping is about clarity and insight. It transforms the abstract concept of 'a network' into a tangible, actionable strategy, providing a visual representation of the connections between individuals across various layers of an organization. This visualization is not limited to external stakeholders but extends into the internal structure of your own organization and will reveal the critical interdependencies and influence patterns that might otherwise remain invisible.

Let's consider a scenario that underscores the value of relationship mapping in B2B selling. Imagine you're targeting a major prospect account: a giant in the industry with the potential to significantly boost your organization's revenue. A traditional sales approach might lead you to focus solely on a small number of direct contacts. However, with a relationship map you build the complete picture, and through some intelligence uncover that the real influencer is a new senior executive in a different part of the organization. You then find out that this person previously worked with the Chief Executive Officer (CEO) as well as discovering that one of your own team members has a university connection with this executive. Suddenly, you have a pathway that wasn't visible before; a strategy informed by the deeper understanding of relationships that this type of mapping provides.

But the power of relationship mapping isn't confined to external sales efforts. It is equally powerful internally too. Consider this same deal but think about all the different teams that need to come together internally. Success will depend on the seamless coordination of many, including marketing, sales, support, procurement, management and perhaps other internal service lines. Having an internal relationship map will reveal the key players in each department which will bring clarity to the strategy, inform leadership and uncover potential bottlenecks in communication and decision-making processes. It's like having a blueprint of your organizational dynamics, enabling you to navigate with confidence and strategic foresight.

Collaboration sits at the heart of an organization's success, whether that is internally to serve the client best or externally with the client to deliver the desired outcomes. A compelling illustration of this in action is seen in the experience of a global professional services organization who recognized that taking a one-firm approach to clients would yield significant benefits, but were unable to operationalize this. They introduced a strategic move to enhance internal collaboration, but it also helped to pinpoint disconnected employees and streamline the process of engaging with existing customers. The analysis used internal data sources such as email logs, calendar invites, chat interactions and Salesforce teaming to provide a granular view of the relationships between internal executives and clients. This allowed the organization to monitor the evolution of these relationships over time and confirm the effectiveness of cross line of service collaboration. The results demonstrated, with quantifiable data points, that where collaboration happened the client was served better, with an improved client experience. In addition, internal executives could be properly compensated for the organization's increased revenue brought about from better collaboration.

This previous example shows the depth and breadth of what is possible from a more advanced application of ONA (Organizational Network Analysis), but as we venture through this chapter, we are invited to explore the profound impact of relationship mapping through a simpler and more practical lens. Taking the hands-on approach that is described in this book will reframe your thinking to expand and visualize relationships in a much broader way, thus setting you up to thrive in the increasingly complex world of business.

Relationship mapping: What it is and what it isn't

Before we examine the process of building a relationship map, it is very useful to understand the context from which this idea was created. The concept was born from two distinct disciplines, namely **social network analysis** and **stakeholder theory**. The first, social network analysis, explains and visualizes how and why different contacts are connected. The second, stakeholder theory, focuses on the interconnected nature of relationships that involves a process of identifying a specific set of stakeholders and then spending time to understand how they impact one another.

Both concepts are discussed in detail in the proceeding sections of this chapter. As will become evident these are two advanced techniques used to identify, analyse and evaluate relationships and are more commonly applied in large and more complex scenarios.

The origins of relationship mapping

Social network analysis

We are all familiar with platforms such as Facebook and LinkedIn, which are examples of social network analysis in action. So, the concept of social networks is already engrained in our day-to-day lives and where there are relationships and connections there is the opportunity to conduct social network analysis. This insight seeks to **understand patterns of relationships between parties,** either on an individual or group level, and to illustrate and explain clusters of relationships. When this is done in a closed group within one organization, it is called **ONA**.

We owe this concept to the work of Jacob Moreno[9] who is credited as first introducing the concept of **visualizing a network in the form of a diagram,** which bore the term sociogram. He was interested in social relationships and their interconnections and wanted to understand the power formations, how cliques are formed and to identify and observe the leaders. The first areas for observation were hospitals and schools. Moreno was interested in the dynamics of small groups and used social network analysis to analyse patterns of communication and influence within these groups. He asked group members to rate their level of attraction to others within the group and used this data to create the first visual representations of the data, called **sociograms**. This illustrated the social structure of the group.

Moreno then applied his work on social networks to the wider community, using social network analysis to understand the structure of social networks in different neighbourhoods. His objective was to **identify key opinion leaders** and then develop effective strategies for community engagement and dissemination of information. So, as we may have gathered from these examples, the input data for social network analysis and sociograms can be sourced in a variety of ways, including surveys, interviews, observations and analysing interaction data. See Figure 3.1 for an example of a sociogram. The leap into the mainstream came with the advent of technological tools that permitted the consumption and visualization of social network data. This was the real breakthrough as it allowed the analysis of huge datasets to happen automatically.

Having a basic understanding of how to create a sociogram will help you later when you are creating your own relationship map. This is because you will be able to visualize in your own mind who the key people are and with whom they are aligned, and this context will help you to see how they fit together in the whole scheme of things. So, while you read the rest of this section try to pause and think about how these different terms relate to actual networks you are aware of, either in your personal or professional life.

Sociograms are usually constructed with 'lines' connecting 'dots'. A dot represents an individual relationship (this could be an individual, an organization or another entity) while the means by which dots are connected are the lines, and these can also be one of two types. First, undirected, meaning there is no directional flow denoted for the relationship – it simply signifies that there is a connection. Second, directed, which allows the flow of a relationship to be illustrated, for example, in social media parlance 'who is "following" who'. **The width of the line between dots represents the strength of the relationship.** There can be a key to explain the width and different colours as part of the sociogram, with aspects such as emotional connection, levels of reciprocity and type/frequency of interactions driving the width of lines and colours. It is the analysis of these dots and lines that provides insights into the social network, and there are many interpretations that can be drawn.

- A 'structural hole' is the absence of a line between two social networks, so there is no means for them to connect.

- A line that connects two dots from two otherwise unconnected networks is called a 'bridge'. The dot managing the bridge is in the advantageous

FIGURE 3.1 Example of a sociogram

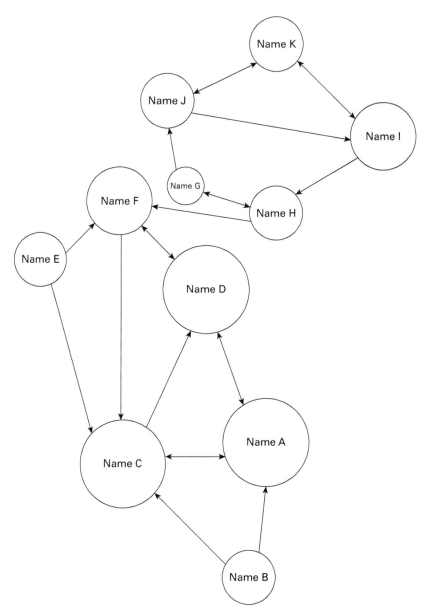

position of being the only one having a view into both networks and, thus, having access to this information. Such a view can provide a competitive advantage on an individual level as well as an advantage from the group's perspective, as this dot is the conduit for the information. This is about who your bridges are, in both your professional and personal lives.

- The '**distance**' is the minimum number of lines required to connect two given dots. This concept was made popular by the work of Travers and Milgram[10] in their concept of 'six degrees of separation', the idea being that any two people anywhere on earth can be connected by six relationships or less.

- **Propinquity** (or nearness): where people are more likely to form bonds with other people who are in close proximity.
- **Homophily** (or sameness): asserting that people are attracted to other people who look, think and behave like them.
- **Multiplexity** (multiples): there will likely be a stronger bond between individuals who can interact on multiple personal (e.g. yoga, coffee shop or pub) and professional (e.g. work, associations or events) levels.
- **Reciprocity**: where people are likely to respond positively to a positive act.
- **Transitivity** (or relational): the premise being that my friend's friend, who I do not know, is more likely to be my friend once we get introduced, as compared to a random person. This is the premise of LinkedIn; to unveil relationships based on homophily, propinquity, multiplexity and transitivity.

So, by consuming these few pages you now have a good grounding in the concept of social network analysis and some of the key terms that explain why and how people associate together, or not as the case may be. This next section examines the second discipline, that of stakeholder theory.

Stakeholder theory

The concept of stakeholder theory emphasizes the importance of identifying and analysing stakeholders. This concept was first introduced by Edward Freeman.[11] Rather than focusing on the desires of shareholders, Freeman's idea was that **organizations should consider the interests of all stakeholders.** These include those who provide inputs to support the organization in the process of creating their product or service, such as employees and suppliers. However, they also include all the output channels, those who help them sell, such as customers and partners. He extended this to include the community around which the organization was based. Once the needs of each stakeholder group were understood, strategies were developed to balance any conflicting interests, which in the long term should result in better outcomes for the organization.

The first step in this process is **identifying all the stakeholders** that have an interest in or are affected by a particular project or situation, and then **categorizing them according to their level of importance and power**. The next step is to **develop strategies to engage with them** effectively to understand their interests, needs and expectations. As discussed later in this book, by understanding and prioritizing stakeholder needs and interests organizations can build trust that results in stronger relationships and enhances their long-term sustainability and success. Freeman's early use cases for stakeholder theory were primarily in the field of strategic management and organizational leadership. Notably, they all evaluated how different entities (rather than individuals) interacted with one another. There are many more examples of his work over the years, but three are summarized below:

1 Freeman analysed the stakeholder relationships of a British supermarket chain. It was known to have a strong brand reputation and maintained very strong customer loyalty. Freeman wanted to explain how and why this was the case, so he used stakeholder theory to map stakeholder relationships. Next, the supermarket mapped the stakeholders to identify key stakeholders and their needs and interests. They then developed a range of stakeholder engagement strategies including regular meetings with suppliers and employees as well as community engagement initiatives. This demonstrated how the supermarket had spent time to build strong relationships with its suppliers, employees and customers, and how this contributed to the organization's success.

2 Freeman approached this use case from a different angle. It was centred on a tragic incident in the 1980s when several people died after taking medication that had been laced with poison. The manufacturer found themselves in the midst of a major crisis that could have threatened their future, but the response was a textbook example of effective crisis management. The organization took immediate steps to recall all of the brand's capsules and worked closely with the media and government agencies to keep the public informed. As the Freeman case study demonstrated, the pharmaceutical company effectively identified all stakeholders and their priorities and were committed to working transparently and collaboratively with them. In doing so they were able to regain the trust of the public and maintain their market-leading position.

3   The premise of Freeman's work is that engaging with and considering the needs of all the stakeholders impacted, both positively and negatively, will result in the best long-term outcome for the organization. So, Freeman examined an energy company's decision-making process for oil exploration and production in the North Sea. These operations were very controversial as they had significant environmental impacts, and there was a lot of resistance from local communities and environmental groups. Freeman's position was that because the company failed to engage effectively with all stakeholders it led to negative outcomes for both it and the wider community, and this damaged its brand and reputation. In more recent times we have seen oil and gas companies invest a lot of time and money repositioning themselves as energy companies with much more of a focus on the environment as well as integrating themselves into the local communities.

As mentioned, Freeman's initial use cases were at an organizational rather than individual level. It is useful to have this grounding and to understand the depth and complexity for which these concepts were originally created, in particular, understanding the needs and interests of the impacted stakeholders so that when we apply this to our more simplified use cases, we have a solid framing to use.

Organizational charts

I have mentioned relationship maps a lot so far and as you will discover later in Part 2, the basis for the relationship map is an organizational chart (org chart). As such, in addition to the two relationship concepts, I also want to explain a bit of the history of the org chart, which is also known as an organogram or hierarchy chart. I was unable to find one particular person who invented the org chart, but the concept dates back to the early 1900s and one of the pioneers in this area was Henri Fayol,[12] a French mining engineer and management theorist. His influential book, *General and Industrial Management*, was published in 1916, and in it Fayol outlined the principles of management, including the concept of how companies were organized. He emphasized the need for clear organizational structures and suggested that a visual representation of the hierarchy could help with this understanding.

Around the same time, other management theorists such as Frederick Winslow Taylor[13] and Max Weber[14] were also developing ideas related to organizational structures. Taylor focused on scientific management and the division of labour while Weber introduced the concept of bureaucracy and hierarchy. The actual use of visual representations to depict organizational structures came with the growing complexity of organizations and subsequently the need for a clear depiction of roles, responsibilities and reporting relationships.

Relationship mapping in the context of this book

In the previous sections we saw the complexity of the scenarios for which social network analysis, sociograms and stakeholder theory and maps were originally created. They were applied to understand and explain how different entities interacted with one another to explain various outcomes. It is important to bring that 'big picture' perspective to the table when we view this in the context of this book. The purpose of this section is, therefore, to help you to visualize in your own mind the complexity of the relationships between various stakeholders as it relates to the three defined use cases:

- Applied to key deals
- Applied to key projects
- Applied to key accounts

These use cases zoom in further, getting to an individual relationship level to identify the specific individuals, research them, create a visualization to map where they all fit and, crucially, execute an engagement strategy to achieve the stated objective. In the context of this book, these stated objectives are all underpinned by delivering commercial outcomes for your organization, to protect, maintain or grow revenue.

So, let us apply what we discussed in the last section to the holistic view of the different stakeholders involved in delivering against these three use cases. In its simplest form, there would be two stakeholders at the group level: your organization (the supplier) and the client organization. At this stage we will not overcomplicate things by including others, for example, external partners. We can explore this further to showcase how quickly this can become very complex. While we go through this section, it will help for you to visualize a scenario in your head – so, think about a job role (past or present) and a client you were working with at that time.

There are two parts to this. The first is the internal stakeholder's side, which is **the view from within your organization** and understanding the relationship you have with each of the internal people within each of these internal departments. I know you are probably in a team, whether that is a team responsible for selling to or managing clients, but that is not your team is it? These are peers, often people who have the same job role as you. Your team is the team that makes you successful in your job. **Your team is the wider ecosystem across your organization**, a combination of technical support people, delivery people, account and salespeople, marketing, business development and product and service line specialists, not to mention finance, legal and your leadership. Thus, the individuals within each of these departments make up 'your team'.

So, what is the relationship you have with your team? If you were thinking about this in the context of social network theory, having done this analysis and each dot was a person, and these dots were clustered together in groups signifying each internal department, **what would your internal sociogram look like?** It is useful for you to do an internal audit to try to visualize where your strongest and weakest relationships lie, and also where there is no real relationship at all.

The second part to this is **your organization's relationship with a particular client**. When you think about such a relationship, clients will also be interacting with the departments just discussed while within each department there is an actual person having the relationship with an actual person on the client side. It is the entirety of all these relationships that forms the complete picture. Now let us think back to Chapter 2 where I laid out the qualities that contribute to trust and just pick one of those items, that of **being effective**. This means making things happen, knowing how to get things done and knowing who to talk to, crucially, both internally within your own organization and on the client side. As we try to navigate our way around these very complex networks, hopefully you can start to see where your strengths and weaknesses lie. In addition, with the application of what we learned in Chapter 2 consider what, specifically, you need to do to improve the quality of the most important internal and external relationships.

With that being said, this is really a situation of controlling the controllables. Even in what might be a simple scenario, when you consider the internal and external relationships it can very quickly become very complex. So, let us stay focused on the outcomes, which for this book are the three use cases.

Introducing the three use cases: key deals, key projects and key accounts

Effectively mapping relationships starts with the premise that unless you know who you are supposed to be influencing, how can you be successful? As such, understanding the network of individuals involved in a particular decision is key. Crucially, by doing this you can **identify the strengths and weaknesses within the network** and can communicate with these parties and foster opportunities for collaboration. You can identify who is with you, who you need to convince and who might be against you. Once you have this view, the risks and threats to your organization become clearer, and you are able define a plan and effectively communicate to management where you are and who is going to do what. Consequently, the strategy to be successful is more robust and, most importantly, you can clearly communicate it.

The three core use cases that this book is anchored around are sequential in nature. If we imagine how any typical company is organized there is a focus on winning new clients, and this is usually focused on a specific set of named prospects or a grouping of industry and/or regional sectors. Once an initial deal is won (use case 1 – key deals), the focus shifts to delivering an exceptional outcome for this new client (use case 2 – key projects). Depending on how your company is organized, whether it means this new account is formally part of an account management structure, a key account that might become part of the strategic account programme or something else, a decision is made to grow the revenue in this new account (use case 3 – key accounts). Underpinning use case 3 is repeating the cycle again by winning the next deal (use case 1 – key deals) and delivering a great outcome (use case 2 – key projects).

However, use case 3 also involves the strategic overlay that comes with growing an account, with a specific focus on effectively identifying, managing and leveraging the relationships at an organizational level within this client account. Each use case will be discussed in detail in Part 3, with one chapter dedicated to each and including case studies. The rest of this chapter will present the specific value that can be gained by having strong relationships within the client organization for each use case.

Winning key deals: Why map relationships?

Winning key deals is the cornerstone of any organization's success. These are the deals that have the financial impact to move the needle within your organization and to make a statement to the market, the industry and your competition. Thus, identifying and defining a pathway to success for key deals is paramount. The following are some of the benefits of mapping and nurturing relationships to be better positioned in key deals:

- **Identifying the key decision makers:** understanding who the key decision makers are on the deal as well as the underlying dynamics and agendas can mean the difference between winning and losing a deal. The best source of this information is directly from within the client organization. This insight and direction from conversations you have with people will drive the strategy and support a positive outcome.

- **Influencing the key decision makers:** these influencers will hold significant sway over the final outcomes and decisions, so building and nurturing relationships with them will substantially increase your chances of success. Through building relationships with these people, understanding their perspectives, needs and priorities, you will be able to effectively tailor your approach and offerings to align with their expectations. Notably, without their support it is unlikely you will win the deal.

- **Insight into the competitive landscape:** one threat to winning a key deal is the competitive landscape. Who else does the organization work with? Who is the incumbent supplier? Who else is bidding? And who internally is supporting them? What does that dynamic look like? Answers to these questions can usually only come from insight through the conversations you are having within the client organization. By recognizing who the key competitors are you are better equipped to position your solution more effectively, differentiate it from competitors and emphasize the unique value it brings to the table. Relationship maps will not only help you identify who has potential insight into who the competitors are but will also help you to identify adversaries who are aligned with competitors.

- **Understanding organizational culture:** an aligned culture was highlighted in Chapter 2 as being a key contributing factor in building trust. It therefore follows that by getting insight directly from conversations with the people you have mapped out, you will be able to understand their cultural nuances. From this you will be able to tailor your approach, messaging and solutions to better resonate with the stakeholders and, ideally, demonstrate that the cultures are aligned. This understanding enables you to align your offerings with the organization's values, ethics and overarching mission, thereby establishing a stronger connection and building trust.

- **Knowing which market and industry trends are important:** demonstrating market and industry knowledge was highlighted in Chapter 2 as being a key contributing factor in building trust. Stakeholders on the client side will often possess valuable insight into market and industry trends they are concerned with and any emerging technologies that they view as having a significant impact on their business. By building relationships with individuals on the client side, you will get details on this thinking which will permit you to demonstrate your awareness of these dynamics as they relate specifically to your client. You will then establish credibility and position your offerings as a competitive advantage. This knowledge allows you to articulate your offering as a solution to these challenges or opportunities, thus demonstrating your understanding of industry trends, showcasing your thought leadership, expertise and ability to provide strategic solutions.

- **Understanding the decision-making criteria:** the decision-making criteria are different in every organization, and in fact, can vary among the decision makers on the same deal. Understanding what these unique factors are is crucial to engaging and persuading them effectively. The only real way to get insight into the decision-making criteria is to build relationships and have conversations with people within the client organization. Relationship maps will help you to target the right people for the right conversations. Each stakeholder may prioritize different aspects such as cost, quality, sustainability or specific business objectives. Knowing this and tailoring your approach allows you to make a more compelling case for your offerings, addressing their individual pain points and presenting the value proposition in a manner that directly aligns with their decision-making criteria.

- **Knowing about allocation of budget:** clearly, knowing if and when funding is available and the process to release it is fundamental to winning a key deal, and a relationship map will provide the route to this insight. By establishing relationships with the key stakeholders responsible for this, it will give you a clear understanding into the organization's financial situation, the processes and any other competing priorities. You can thereby align your solution, pricing, payment terms, and thus your total value propositions to their budget and timelines. This will also help you to manage internal expectations on when the deal will close.

- **Understanding the timing of the deal:** knowing the timelines the client is working to is paramount for successful pipeline management, and your internal credibility is often impacted by this. As such, recognizing that the key client stakeholders can provide you with a deeper understanding of the timing and urgency on their side is key to your success. By having a well-built map, good relationships and maintaining open lines of communication you can get up-to-date information on this, especially if timelines are changing for the worse.

- **Contract negotiation:** having trust with the key executives and deep understanding of clients' priorities and preferences will allow you to better understand their risk appetite, address their concerns and anticipate potential objections, desired contractual terms and potential areas of flexibility. The relationship map will enable you to identify the right people to work with to craft an agreement that aligns with their expectations and increases the likelihood of successful contract negotiations. This insight will come from solid and trusting relationships and if things get tense, as they often do, then it is even more important to have built up that level of rapport and trust to get over those final hurdles.

Delivering key projects: Why map relationships?

The crucial part of this whole process is the delivery, especially if these are key projects in the early stage of the relationship. Gaining a deeper understanding of the project and its stakeholders will help you to develop targeted strategies to ensure the success of the project by first delivering business value and then having the opportunity to grow revenue. We have considered all of the effort that goes into winning a key deal, so that same focus and attention needs to be applied to the project to ensure that it does not fail. This is all dependent on the quality of information, which itself is dependent on the quality of the relationships. The following are some of the key benefits of mapping and nurturing relationships to better manage key projects:

- **Identifying key stakeholders on the project:** as with the key deal use case, one of the first things you need to do is to identify the key decision makers, or in this case the key stakeholders. If you are not sure who the important players are in the project, the ones who determine whether the project is a success or not, then it will be very difficult to make the project a success. Who these people are can be found out by talking to people within the project team as well as within the wider organization. This will enable the project teams to identify the key players and their respective roles, allowing for effective research and intelligence gathering, coordination and collaboration throughout the project.

- **Identifying key stakeholder and project priorities:** having a comprehensive understanding of stakeholder and project needs, interests and priorities enables the project team to align to these, and it will dramatically increase the likelihood of a successful outcome. So, by defining and then prioritizing stakeholder requirements and aligning to project goals accordingly, the project team lays the foundations for success, gets stakeholder engagement and creates a favourable project environment. This insight is gleaned through conversations and building strong relationships within the client organization.

- **Improved project communication:** as discussed in Chapter 2, the flow of information and how honest clients are with us is linked to how much they trust us and whether sufficient opportunity to build 'mutual disclosure' has occurred. As such, the success of any key project relies heavily on effective communication. Project teams need to have the right quality of relationship with the right people, to then be able to identify the most appropriate communication channels for each stakeholder and tailor the style to their preferences. This personalized approach ensures that all stakeholders are engaged and actively contributing to the project's success. Some of the outcomes of having strong relationships that permit high levels of open and transparent communication are the ability to mitigate project risks, identify bottlenecks and other issues, and to highlight additional requirements or enhancements that will increase the likelihood of project success.

- **Customer satisfaction and customer retention:** the outcome of any project is to deliver value to the client organization, and this should have been defined and agreed at the beginning and the progress mapped throughout the project lifecycle. As discussed, having good-quality relationships allows for communication to be open, and feedback and guidance to be shared so there is limited opportunity for misunderstandings and misalignments. By actively investing in these relationships project teams can enhance stakeholder satisfaction, promote loyalty and establish a solid foundation for future collaborations and opportunities beyond the project's completion.

Growing key accounts: Why map relationships?

The final and arguably the most significant of the three use cases is growing key accounts. It is often said that 80 per cent of revenue comes from

20 per cent of clients, so it makes sense to manage key clients with a different sense of purpose. Use case 1 – key deals and use case 2 – key projects will both play an important role in use case 3 – key accounts. This is because to be effective in managing a key account you will need to close key deals and make key projects successful.

All of the benefits already mentioned in use cases 1 and 2 apply here, but at the core of any successfully managed key account is having a good understanding of who has access to key information and who are the power players within the client organization. The earlier you are aware of something significant happening and who is driving it, the quicker you can respond. So, by understanding these intricate networks you are able to identify the key decision makers and influencers. Having sight of this information is important and at the root of this is having access to reliable information sourced from quality relationships. This understanding permits many different types of insight to be gleaned, as follows:

- **Monitoring and adapting to C-suite priorities:** aligning to the organizational priorities of the client you serve is key to your success, and having good relationships with the right individuals will permit you direct access to what is going on internally. Priorities change or can become more defined, but whatever the case the sooner you have access to this information the sooner you can adapt the messaging and solutions to better suit these needs. The quality of this information is linked to the quality of your relationships. In referring to the C-suite, this includes the CEO, Chief Financial Officer (CFO) and Chief Operating Officer (COO).

- **Knowing about key role changes and reorganization:** obtaining information about people coming into new roles, either external hires or people moving internally, is useful and can prove instrumental in winning new business and also getting insight into potential threats to existing business. Having good information and building quality relationships helps you to understand the key stakeholders' expectations, their preferences and their motivations, thus enabling you to tailor the engagement strategies and solutions accordingly.

- **Partner ecosystem and cross-functional collaboration:** when trust and credibility with key stakeholders is established it makes it easier to effectively engage with other internal departments as well as the wider partner ecosystem. People in large organizations are often working in silos, and insight gained as a result of the quality of a variety of relationships can provide an excellent opportunity to help connect the dots.

- **Developing and delivering a strong value proposition:** this flow of information allows you to understand the internal dynamic and the key priorities, to gather critical information and to validate assumptions. In turn, this will enable you to develop and deliver solutions that continue to meet the clients' expectations. Strong and open relationships also provide opportunities for ongoing and honest feedback and while this type of feedback is rare it is critical to ensuring what you are doing is delivering maximum value. It also allows for the opportunity to create customized solutions and services.

- **Managing risk:** strong relationships contribute to honest and transparent discussions where you can openly discuss potential risks and challenges. This facilitates early identification of issues and allows for collaborative problem solving and contingency planning. It allows for constructive dialogues about performance metrics, progress and areas for improvement. Where a strong relationship exists, the client is more likely to provide accurate feedback and share insights that can address challenges and create solid contingency plans.

What we've learned in this chapter

We have learned three key things in this chapter:

- What relationship mapping means.
- The origins of relationship mapping.
  - Social network analysis.
  - Stakeholder engagement.
- Why relationship maps help to win key deals, manage key projects and develop key accounts.

What's coming next

Part 1 is complete, so you now have a solid foundational understanding of the what, the why and the how of relationships and the history of relationship mapping. Next is Part 2, which devotes a chapter to each of the three steps to building a relationship map.

PART TWO

An overview of how to build and execute a relationship map

The next three chapters form Part 2 of this book and will take you through the three-step process to build and execute a relationship map, as follows:

- Chapter 4 covers the initial identification and mapping of the key stakeholders.
- Chapter 5 explains how to conduct effective desktop research and intelligence gathering on the identified key stakeholders.
- Chapter 6 describes the process to engage with the key stakeholders and others who can help with intelligence.

Putting these steps into action will take time and effort. Indeed, it may take more than you would usually spend on such things, but after one cycle through this three-step process the rewards will be clear to see. You will have more clarity and will be able to make better decisions which will result in better outcomes. The process is designed to be initially applied in three specific scenarios:

- Key deals: the big deals that matter to you and your organization.
- Key projects: perhaps a must-win pilot or a top-priority project for a new or existing client.
- Key accounts: your most strategic accounts.

Once a relationship map has been put into place and results are seen within one or more of the above use cases, it then gets ingrained into the day to day. It will become second nature and will be infused into all key deals, key projects and key accounts. This book is designed to be used by one individual for the deals, projects and accounts they are working on. It will explain how you can put this into action and also how you can showcase the progress to (and involve) your internal team, your leadership and the wider organization. In practice you will probably be working in a bid team, project team or key account team, and others will be contributing to the process.

Nothing more than an internet connection and access to the typical business software such as LinkedIn, Microsoft Excel and PowerPoint or the Google equivalents is required. For ease of explaining and understanding the basics I have tried to simplify the process and the steps within. Access to any additional software is not required, but there will be signposts in the places where organizations that have deployed this on a broader scale have used paid software to make the whole process more effective and scalable.

The process is very detailed and provides an in-depth, step-by-step guide as to how to identify stakeholders, conduct research and intelligence gathering on them and finally how to engage with them. You will already be familiar with a lot of this and will also already be putting some of it into action. The added benefit of this book is that it will provide you with a solid process to apply. At first it will take time to build up the data that you need, so prioritize your own use cases and keep up the momentum as best you can.

So, read through everything and pick out what will work best for you based on the time you have and the importance of the deal. For example, I was part of a team working on a deal worth over $100 million, with several colleagues staying in hotels in different cities for months (travelling home Friday to Monday). I was working full time on only this one deal and in that scenario I had time to focus on each and every step of the process. However, this has not always been the case, and we all have to make judgement calls on which steps will deliver the biggest impact in the timeframe available.

Before you start to create anything it is important to read the whole book. Part 3, Putting the relationship-mapping process into action, explains with practical detail how this can all fit together within your key deals (Chapter 7), key projects (Chapter 8) and/or key accounts (Chapter 9). The book finishes with Chapter 10 where I spend time explaining how to implement this process end to end, including at organizational level.

I have templates and other resources to help you to implement this process. Please contact me via www.ryan-osullivan.com and I will be happy to share them at no cost.

Introducing the three-step process

While these steps are sequential they will need repeating as new information becomes available, so it is a **living, iterative process** that requires going back and forth between steps.

Step 1 – initial mapping of relationships – has **five elements** to it. It starts with 1a understanding and aligning to **client priorities**, and then 1b takes that information to develop a **strategy for success**. Next, 1c asks you to start to think about the **relationship strategy** for this deal, project or account while with 1d we finally get to start **identifying stakeholders**. This step is like a relationship audit of everyone that is known by the deal or project team (and wider within the organization). Considering that each key stakeholder plays a significant role, it is important to get all of this detail out and into one place. Then you have a foundation from which to strategize and execute a plan. Once you have this information we can move on to 1e which is **building an org chart**. This foundational layer forms the basis from which to work and to support the strategy on a key deal, key project or key account.

Step 2 – research and intelligence gathering – also has **five elements**. From Part 1 we have clearly understood the important role thorough research and intelligence gathering plays in the relationship-building process. Doing this properly is how you will distinguish yourself from the rest. Therefore, 2a is desktop research which focuses on the identified stakeholder's **social media channels** while 2b focuses on **other public sources** of insight. Next, 2c is gathering intelligence from **people who used to work** at the target organization. At this point we switch from desktop research to actually talking to people to gather intelligence 'from the field'. As such, 2d is **talking to partners and other external parties** while in 2e we talk to **people currently**

FIGURE 4.1 Introducing the three-step process

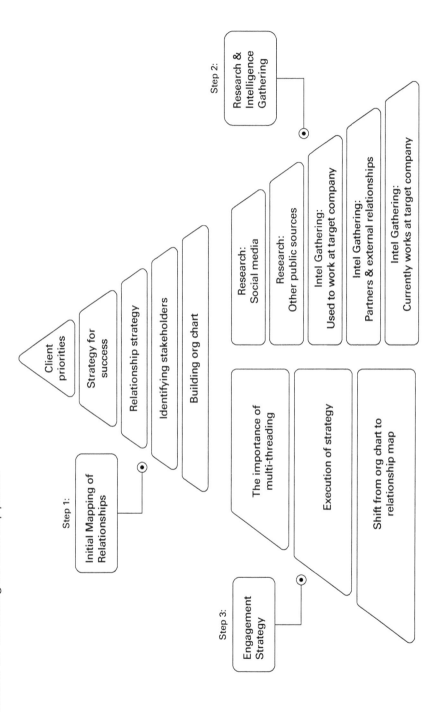

working at the target organization, which is the crux of where the intelligence gathering will happen.

Step 3 – engagement strategy – has **three elements** and explains how to define, implement and execute the strategy. It starts with 3a which discusses the importance of **multi-threading** in this process while 3b is the **execution of the engagement strategy**. This is when, based on what we now know, we can define who from within your organization will reach out to who, via what channel and for what purpose, and then do it! Finally, 3c explains how we now shift from a one-dimensional **org chart to a relationship map.** Figure 4.1 introduces the three-step process in diagrammatic form.

4

How to build and execute a relationship map: Step 1, initial mapping of relationships

Introduction

MANISH MALHOTRA, INFOSYS – VICE PRESIDENT OF SALES (FINANCIAL SERVICES EMEA) & COUNTRY CO-HEAD OF INFOSYS UK

When managing a deal, project or account, it's common to focus exclusively on the individuals you interact with regularly. However, this narrow approach can expose you to significant risks and cause you to miss substantial opportunities. This chapter will discuss how to avoid the pitfalls of narrow engagement by broadening your line of sight to include a wider range of stakeholders. By visualizing this you can then pinpoint the gaps and develop strategies to build new relationships. When such effort is aligned with your clients' priorities, this broader engagement will elevate your role from a 'just another supplier' to a strategic partner. This is because you and your organization are positioned better with the newly identified key executives.

Over the years I have observed this issue countless times, but one particular client experience brings this to light. The layout of their head office was telling, with the IT and back-office teams being positioned in one part of the building while the C-suite executives and business teams were in another. Notably, our engagement was confined to dealing with the IT and back-office people and although we had visited the office many times, we had rarely been into the 'business' side of the building. But this client did generate significant revenue for us and we delivered quality and highly valued work so, on the face of it, it was a successful client.

However, once we took the time to map out the entire organization we identified gaps not only in our relationships but also, crucially, in our ability to understand our client's business priorities. Realizing this we made a deliberate and painstaking effort to build relationships with the business teams. This strategic shift transformed our relationship, eventually earning us a seat at the executive table and us being involved in and shaping their corporate priorities. At this point we were viewed as a strategic partner.

This gap (and opportunity) was only uncovered when we identified and mapped the key stakeholders against our current relationships, which shone a light on how isolated we were in the whole scheme of things. So, ask yourself these same questions in relation to your own strategic deals and accounts. As you go through this chapter – and the rest of the book – you will explore the techniques for identifying and mapping out the key stakeholder landscape. By doing so you will gather valuable insights to allow you to align with the priorities and concerns of senior decision makers, thus helping to solidify your position as a valued partner.

The elements of mapping relationships

This chapter will discuss the separate elements of relationship mapping, in turn, and as they are introduced it will become apparent that they form part of a continuous cycle. So, perhaps you realize you are lacking detail in one area, but that is okay. You can continue through the three-step process for other areas and will have the opportunity to fill those gaps in the next iteration.

While 1c (relationship strategy), 1d (identifying stakeholders) and 1e (building an org chart) fit squarely as the core focus of this book, it's less so for client priorities and strategy for success. There are entire books devoted to understanding and aligning to client priorities and developing and executing on strategies to be successful (win strategies). However, they are both mentioned here because they are central to success, whether that is with a key deal, a key project or a key account.

Step 1a: Client priorities

We built this storyline throughout Part 1, and especially in Chapter 2, but it's worth highlighting again the foundational significance of having a good understanding of – and aligning to – client priorities. Not least, this leads to a deeper understanding of the client. While learning about client priorites will be an ongoing iterative process, it makes sense to start this whole process off with this in mind as without this understanding, nothing else matters. It is okay to not have this insight yet, as the three-step process will guide you on how to get it. This type of insight can be at the organizational level, but also at the industry segment level, service line level, regional level and indeed at the team and individual levels. In an ideal world, a good understanding across all of these would be advantageous.

A client's strategic priorities and objectives tend to be their focal point and something that the whole organization rallies around. So, to understand their priorities is to understand the client. When there is acknowledgement from the client that you have this clarity, the **rapport-building** process is smoother and **trust** can start to form. This leads to more **open communication** and by using language that resonates with the client's priorities it builds further confidence and trust in the supplier. Next is the opportunity for the supplier to bring **value-adding insights**. By bringing relevant case studies, best practice or other industry or market insights that are linked to delivering against the client priorities, the supplier can position themselves as more of a **trusted adviser**. This enhances **credibility** and better positioning in the client ecosystem.

When this level of relationship exists, **proactive problem solving** can occur where the client will trust your perspective to anticipate potential challenges and obstacles they may face. Tied in with this is **anticipating future needs** of their business which is when it might make sense to start to position your own solutions. Where appropriate there should be **bespoke solutions** tailored to their objectives and business outcomes, the result being that your solution is better tied to the business priorities and superior when compared to the competition.

This all happens from the anchor point of aligning with and delivering to the client priorities. From there the relationship becomes stronger and stronger, and as these cycles continue there is a shift from the supplier-client relationship to the trusted adviser status and a co-dependency on one another as part of an integrative B2B relationship. However, there is a big leap from understanding client priorities to being successful, whether that is winning a key deal, making a key project successful or growing a key account. The central argument this book is making is that the quality of the key relationships sits at the heart of your ability to get to the detail required to be successful.

Step 1b: The strategy for success

As the client priorities come from the client side, the strategy that will make your organization successful comes from the value proposition positioned from the supplier side. In complex, high-value B2B relationships this strategy is a well-defined plan of action designed to maximize the chances of being successful. It involves a comprehensive approach that considers the unique dynamics, challenges and stakeholders involved in the decision. The purpose of a success strategy is to position the supplier as the preferred choice and create a compelling case for the client to choose their solution over competitors, or, as is discussed in detail in Dixon and McKenna's book *The JOLT Effect*,[15] the client doing nothing and staying with the status quo. As discussed, the foundation of a successful strategy is understanding the **client priorities** and aligning your solution to **deliver value**. We can now uncover some of the key pieces to making this happen.

This brings us to the **internal team** you have assembled, whether it's the bid team for a key deal, the delivery team for a key project or the account and delivery team for a key account. It's this team that will be expected to build and maintain the relationships with the key people on the client side. The quality of these people and **their ability to integrate into the client organization** and be accepted is important. Indeed, those who have some prior knowledge of the client or some pre- or existing relationships should be prioritized and leveraged. The reason for this is that it's this team and the quality of the information they are able to get that will support the win strategy and ultimately determine success or failure.

One of the core risks to being successful is the **competitive landscape**. Knowing who else is working within the client and which of these might be competition forms an important component of your win strategy. There are **other risks** associated with deals and projects, such as decision making and funding criteria and processes, of which clarity is required. For you to be able to create a **compelling business case**, specific business metrics, key performance indicators (KPIs) and other forms of ROI metrics are needed. These form the backbone to your value proposition, and the quality of this insight is usually directly correlated to the quality of your relationships.

The same is true when it comes to being prepared for **handling objections**. If you know what the key objections to your solution are in advance you are able to navigate them more effectively. The key is to position the **differentiators** and, again, knowing which ones are considered more valuable will help you to focus more on those. Ultimately, a successful win strategy is about effectively communicating an end-to-end **winning value proposition**.

Finally, the end result of any successful win strategy is a bunch of people agreeing to your solution. If you have built up a solid understanding of who these people are and what they are thinking, it is more likely to be achieved. So, these two elements of knowing the client priorities and developing a solid win strategy lead us to the crux of this book: who are the people that can enable us to get the insight we need and what is **the relationship strategy** to make us successful?

Step 1c: The relationship strategy

Everything starts and ends with the relationship strategy. Whether a key deal, key project or key account, it's the relationship strategy that should drive the decision making and next steps. As we'll uncover within the rest of this chapter and then Chapters 5 and 6, everything that we plan and execute is driven by identifying, building or nurturing relationships. Whether those relationships are for intelligence gathering, asking for an introduction or directly talking to a decision maker, it's the relationship strategy that is at the heart. Depending on what stage you are at in the process of understanding the client priorities and developing the win strategy, this will determine where you are with regard to the relationship strategy. Indeed, an initial relationship strategy might be as simple as identifying who you know the best and then going to have an informal conversation with them.

Executing on the relationship strategy is covered in Chapter 6, but it is important that the thinking on the strategy is placed here, so you are considering how you plan to engage. Where will you start? Who will reach out? What will they talk about? There is no need to do any of that right now, that will come as part of Chapter 6, but just start to think about this in relation to the key deal, project or account that you have in mind.

Step 1d: Identify stakeholders

Now we get to the exciting part: the stakeholders! The first action is to identify those stakeholders who have an interest in or are affected by the key deal, key project or key account, the purpose being to create an initial list of the whole universe of stakeholders, including those you have confirmed as being involved as well as others you might not be sure about yet. Once you have identified each stakeholder it's important to determine their roles and responsibilities, and this will help you to understand their influence on the decision-making process and tailor your approach accordingly. You are then able to categorize them according to their level of importance and power.

This involves assessing their influence and impact, their level of interest or concern and, ideally, who is working for who. From this exercise the key decision makers become apparent. There may also be other individuals within the organization who have influence, so it's important to identify all of these to understand the power of their relationship in the decision-making process. We are not reaching out to any of these stakeholders yet, simply pulling together a list of key people, and there are three key ways to start this identification.

The first: published lists

Depending on the size of the client organization, **published lists of the board, leadership or management team** can be found on their website. This usually identifies the C-suite, which is the CEO and all those who directly report to them. It can be a rich source of base information and can assist in organizing the rest of the people under the formal reporting structure. Aside from the usual reports (CFO, COO, etc) this org chart will also uncover some of the details around what is important to the CEO, as these individuals will report directly to them. For example, if there is a president of Americas and a president of rest of world who both report to the CEO, this will tell you that the organization is split into two regions and the presidents focus on their geographic profit-and-loss accounts (beneath them may be country vice-presidents or product line vice-presidents). Some organizations have a Chief Customer Officer and some do not. Some CEOs have a direct human resources (HR) report, others do not. Companies are organized differently, and how they are organized can tell you something about their power structure and culture.

The second: existing knowledge

Utilize the **existing knowledge** you and the extended team can leverage. Whether you have an existing relationship with the stakeholder or in fact have never met them isn't important at this stage; right now it's about identifying them as potentially being a key stakeholder and getting their name on to the list. You can start by trying to get the full context and history of this account. What have you done, with whom and what happened? The purpose is to gather historical information to attain a base knowledge. Indeed, capturing the names of any internal people from your organization will be useful in Step 2 when you start gathering intelligence. For now, you just want to understand who the key stakeholders are as they apply to your key deal, key project or key account. Next, we look at some examples of how this can be achieved, noting that the list isn't exhaustive.

The most common method is through **internal detective work**. This involves piecing together information from various people and internal systems to see who has touched the account in the past. To achieve this, client relationship management (CRM) (also known as customer relationship management) is a good place to start since these systems can act as a data hub and offer the tools required to collate such data on people within organizations. Is it an existing account? If it's a prospect, what is the history? Look at closed opportunities (closed-won and closed-lost) and check out the people associated with these opportunities; as noted above there is often a place to capture who worked on them. As well as seeing who the opportunity owner is, you can often see who else was attached to the opportunity from across your organization, whether that is the horizontal sales teams, technical teams or other cross-functional teams. Gather this information as a starting point and then check who is still around in the organization. However, it's important to note that there will likely be senior people who would not typically be listed in the CRM. So, once you have the base data points ask around a bit more and add these people to the list.

Another method is to deploy the use of **relationship intelligence software**. There is software available in the market which provides a complete view of relationships that are held internally across your organization. One such software is Introhive (full disclosure: at the time of writing this book, Introhive is my current employer). Introhive connects to your organization's mail server and compiles a view of who internally is communicating (via email and calendar appointments) with clients and prospects. Based on the volume of activity and other inputs such as their seniority and reciprocity, it provides a view of the strength of the relationship. From this you will have an easy way to see and, thus, begin to understand who has a relationship within specific target client organizations and, importantly, the strength of that relationship (based on the volume of activity over work email). In this scenario you could identify people internally who have existing relationships with people in the prospect client organization. These relationships have been maintained over work email, so you have talk to them to determine if this was linked to the prior engagements with that organization and, if so, you have to piece together the key stakeholder landscape.

The third: LinkedIn

Identifying key stakeholders to supplement the detail you have already gathered from the published data as well as from internal sources can be done using LinkedIn. If you are not familiar with **LinkedIn** there are many tutorials on the internet that can be accessed via a search engine. The published leadership or management team of the prospect organization gives an organization-wide view. As you start to develop the list of people that matter in your scenario, you can identify these specific people on LinkedIn, and then check their contacts with people in your organization. For example, if you are particularly interested in the finance department this would drive you to focus on developing this part of the relationship map. However, if it was the sales and/or marketing department you would start to get a feel for who fits where, by finding key people and putting them into this initial list within the spreadsheet (or whichever similar system you use). At this stage it does not need to be an exhaustive list; the key thing is to familiarize yourself with some of the key people who sit in the departments that are important to you.

Updating stakeholder details

At this point the current state will be a long list of names, and as you build this list and put it into a useable format you can add more details about each stakeholder. The basic information to capture is the person's **name** and **job title**; however, I like to add in their **geographical location** as this can be useful for analysis later (this can usually be found on their LinkedIn page). Other useful information is the name of the **current relationship holder** who is the person within your organization that holds the relationship. If that isn't established yet, you can leave it blank.

An initial view on the current **relationship quality** is important too. You can develop your own model over time, but if you do not have one perhaps the following can serve you to get started:

- **Strong:** they generally respond when contacted (either by you or the relationship holder). You have had numerous meetings together and have an understanding of their personality and their business.

- **Weak:** still at a superficial level. You have exchanged a few emails and perhaps met once, but you couldn't be sure they'd engage if they were contacted.

- **Negative:** something has happened at either a personal or professional level, and there is a negative feeling towards the relationship holder and/or your organization.

- **Unknown (none):** you are not sure who has a relationship or there is currently no relationship.

The **decision-making power** is also a very important input as it provides some indication on their overall significance. The concept of the buying centre (also referred to as the decision-making unit) was proposed by Webster and Wind,[16] and the process of decision making can cover all the people you are interacting with, from junior to senior. You might already be using tags to define this, use ones that you have seen in other books or you may wish to make up your own that make sense for your organization. Whatever you choose they tend to follow a similar meaning, as follows:

- **Decider:** this role has the authority to make the final decision. Buying decision-making units are complex, and there will often be more than one person who is attributed as a final decision maker. In terms of internal politics, one decision maker may be more powerful than the others, and you have to consider these scenarios carefully.

- **Recommender:** this role often doesn't have the final say, but their expertise is critical in shaping the decision. For example, they might be a subject matter expert or have other types of specialist insight or experience that the decider feels is important.

- **Evaluator:** this is typically someone who has experience with the solution/supplier/product, so is a user of the product or consumer of the service. These people give hands-on insight or feedback that can better inform a decision.

- **Influencer:** someone who may not be directly involved in the decision-making process but does have some form of sway or influence over those making the decision. An influencer may be internal, such as a legal or safety expert, or an external specialist consultant.

- **Unknown:** this is when you are not sure which one to choose and are aware that more research and intelligence gathering needs to be done.

Assessing where their **allegiances** lie on the deal is also a critical factor in your success, and there will probably be a competitive element for any deal, project or account. This can be a direct competitor to your organization (or several), a disrupter (new market entrant), an in-house solution (the client doing the project themselves) or 'do-nothing', where the client decides that they cannot sustain the change management needed to implement the project successfully. For someone to make a decision people need to be fired up to make a change to the status quo; if no one cares then it's likely the outcome could be to do nothing. This can be split into the following four categories:

- **Supporter:** they want to do something and see you as best placed to support them.
- **Detractor:** they want to do something but have a preference to work with another supplier or would like to do it with internal resources. People that don't see this as a problem worth solving would also go into the detractor bucket.
- **Neutral:** they agree something needs to be done but don't have a particular preference for who does it.
- **Unknown:** their preferences and motivations are not known.

> Through this exercise, and as part of the research and intelligence-gathering process in the next chapter, you may also start to uncover signs of **internal politics**. This is when individuals or teams are vying for influence within the organization. It can lead to allegiances and competing factions within an organization, so understanding and navigating this is crucial.

Across relationship strength, decision-making power and allegiance we have the option for **unknown**, and I'd suggest that in a first cycle through this relationship-mapping process there will be a lot of unknowns, and that is perfectly normal. It shows that you don't have this information yet, but it brings into focus what you need to find out; mostly through Step 3 when you finally start talking to people. Finally, I always add a space for **notes** too. This can be anything in particular you want to capture, such as a piece of information someone shares with you on one of the points above or a note to remind yourself of something for later.

It's important to mention that the process of identifying stakeholders is an iterative one, and the list of stakeholders is a living document. You will

FIGURE 4.2 Sample template to identify key stakeholders

	MAP RELATIONSHIPS				RELATIONSHIP STATUS			
Client Individual	Role in Deal/Org	Location	Relationship Holder	Last Interaction	Role in the Decision	Existing Relationship (y/n)	Supporter OR Detractor
name 1	role 1	country/city	name	date	Decider	y/n + notes	Supporter
name 2	role 2	country/city	name	date	Recommender	y/n + notes	Detractor
name 3	role 3	country/city	name	date	Evaluator	y/n + notes	Neutral
name 4	role 4	country/city	name	date	Influencer	y/n + notes	Unknown
name 5	role 5	country/city	name	date	Unknown	y/n + notes	Supporter

experience this as we progress through the next two steps and, indeed, come back to this first step as part of the continuous cycle. Figure 4.2 is an illustration of this data, and the templates I can share use Microsoft Excel or Google Sheets. This would be used as more of an internal template relationships tracker (subsequently referred to as the tracker) for you and the core team rather than something you would share with leadership or the wider team, as there is a lot of data within this sheet. Also note that I use the same tracker for all three steps, so everything is contained within one master document. As I have mentioned these are available for free by contacting me at www.ryan-osullivan.com.

Step 1e: Building an org chart

Choosing your software option

Once we have a list of stakeholders we then need to turn this into a visual representation. While perfectly fine to work from a list of names, creating a visual representation helps to see where each person fits in the overall organizational structure. As such, it helps with **collaboration** and **strategizing** because it's easier to explain and discuss different ideas and plans. These include discussing who is going to do what to who and in which order. In Chapter 3 we saw what a sociogram looks like, but these can be very complex and require specialized software. For the purposes of this book we'll be simplifying this to ensure that implementing the end-to-end relationship-mapping process is as simple and straightforward as possible.

There are many different software options available when it comes to creating an org chart. However, the basic functionality is often similar and you may be more familiar with one over another, with Microsoft Excel or Google Sheets being good options. There are also a number of software suppliers that specialize in creating org charts, and your organization may have licences for these. If not, some offer basic subscriptions for free and include Lucid charts, Organimi, Hundred Handshakes and Altify. LinkedIn has also just come out with their own version, but I do not recommend any particular product mentioned over others not mentioned.

Depending on what software can be made available to you or what you are already using as part of your existing way of working, choose the one you are most comfortable with. Personally, I use a mapping tool from Introhive but before that was available I used Microsoft Excel. So, for the purposes of this step and for rest of this book I'll use Microsoft Excel; however, whatever software you choose it's very easy nowadays to find video tutorials from the internet via a search engine.

Building the chart

Start by using the **hierarchy** you have from the leadership or management team to form the basic structure. There is no need to worry about knowing exactly where people go since this is an iterative process and the chart can be amended as more information is gathered. The goal at this point is to establish a base which will evolve over time.

Once the base has been established you can start to work on **formatting boxes,** which at first may appear to be an insignificant aspect. However, colour coding or changing the line width of the box is a useful way to highlight certain individuals and also signify something about the state of that particular relationship. Indeed, the simple act of doing this can help to inform other aspects such as the hierarchy mentioned above. Some of the colour coding I do includes the width of the line to signify the strength of the relationship, whereby weak is a thinner line while strong is a thicker line. In addition, a green outline to a box signifies a supporter versus a red one for

FIGURE 4.3 Org chart example

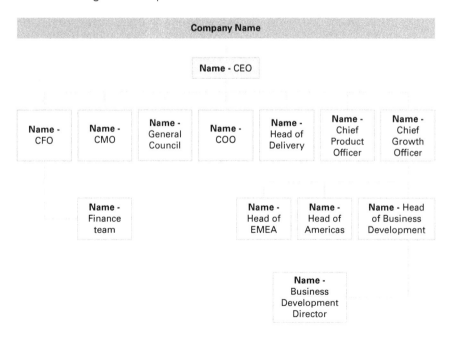

a detractor, and there is a green box for the champion on the client side. However, I do tend to limit the colours and other formatting when sharing with a wider group. See Figure 4.3 for an example of a standard org chart.

> If you are sharing your chart with a wider audience take care as different colours can be distracting. It should be a clean representation of the current status and something you can use as a base to explain your strategy. If being used as part of a meeting then you can voice over the strategy and explain it live.

Capturing and presenting this insight

We've just walked through examples of, first, how you can capture the output from identifying the key stakeholders. This was presented in Microsoft Excel but could just as easily have been completed in any other spreadsheet editor, such as Google Sheets. Secondly, we looked at visualizing the stakeholders in an org chart. Again, this was done using Microsoft Excel but (as discussed) can be done in a variety of ways. I'd always advise experimenting and figuring out what works best for you and your team, as well as the wider organization. There is no right or wrong way, it's just about doing what works best.

For management updates or discussions with a wider team, depending on the audience it might make sense to summarize and copy over details into Microsoft PowerPoint. This can be a cleaner way to work and you can switch to the spreadsheets if needed. The key point is that spreadsheet software works best when you are building and analysing an org chart, but a PowerPoint is usually best when you are presenting it to others.

What we've learned in this chapter

The key things we have learned in this chapter are the five elements to Step 1 (initial mapping of relationships):

- 1a: client priorities.
- 1b: strategy for success.

- 1c: relationship strategy.
- 1d: identify stakeholders.
- 1e: building an org chart.

What's coming next

The next chapter outlines the process for conducting desktop research and gathering intelligence about the organization and the key stakeholders, and is broken into five elements:

- 2a: desktop research – social media.
- 2b: desktop research – other public sources.
- 2c: intelligence gathering – used to work at target organization.
- 2d: intelligence gathering – partners and other external relationships.
- 2e: intelligence gathering – currently works at prospect organization.

5

How to build and execute a relationship map: Step 2, desktop research and intelligence gathering

Introduction

ROSHAN SHETTY, TECH MAHINDRA – BANKING, FINANCIAL
SERVICES & INSURANCE HEAD (AMERICAS)

In Chapter 4 you learnt about the process of identifying the key stakeholders while Chapter 6 will discuss the strategy to engage with them. But when you meet a senior decision maker, if you don't have any value to offer there is little chance of them taking you seriously or treating you on a peer-to-peer level. The key to this is preparation. Abraham Lincoln purportedly remarked (although there is no conclusive evidence) that if he was given six hours to chop down a tree, he would spend the first four sharpening the axe.[17] This encapsulates a profound truth in that the value of preparation cannot be overstated. In fact, in my experience it is the distinguishing factor that will set you apart from the rest, especially when engaging with senior decision makers.

Individuals should constantly be sharpening their knowledge when it comes to having a solid industry, domain or technology perspective. This includes being able to give your point of view on what 'next' means, where the sector or industry is heading or where new threats are going to come from. When you have an important meeting, doing thorough research is table stakes but the pursuit for insights is paramount. Whether that is going through the organization's financial reports and listening to their earnings calls, or reviewing social media and other online material.

However, in my view the biggest opportunity to make an impact comes from having conversations, whether they are with people acquainted with the industry or organizations, the executives you are meeting or the programme. It is these conversions that yield invaluable nuggets of information – insights into priorities and concerns, and the intricate web of internal different viewpoints. It is this intelligence that serves as the key differentiator and will act as the edge that sets you apart from the others and position you favourably in the eyes of the executives.

Consider a competitive pitch to a global organization. Everyone will come in and present their wealth of industry knowledge and a meticulously crafted presentation, and they will all enter the boardroom with confidence. However, be the one who has integrated insights garnered from conversations with the key stakeholders and their direct reports, can anticipate any objections and can align the pitch to their priorities. This will truly capture their attention, earn their respect and ultimately increase the chances of winning the business.

In the chapter that follows, we will delve deeper into the intricacies of this type of research and intelligence gathering. Dr O'Sullivan lays out a solid process for you to follow that will provide the apt structure and direction. It is only through the diligent honing of our preparation that we can hope to navigate the complexities of stakeholder engagement. So, remember Lincoln's quote and I'll finish with one of my favourites from Bobby Unser: 'Success is where preparation and opportunity meet'.[18]

Different types of research

Before we discuss the five elements of Step 2 it will be useful to explain how different types of research fit together to support the relationship-mapping process. There are two types of research: primary, which tends to be when you collect the data directly from the source, such as conducting an interview, and secondary, which is when you collect data that is already published. This chapter is titled 'research and intelligence gathering'. In this chapter, 'research' relates to secondary research which, ironically, is almost always done first. 'Intelligence gathering' is primary research, involving direct discussions with individuals.

Secondary research (also known as desktop research)

Let us start with the research element as it's best to do this before you start talking to people. Desktop research is the process of gathering information and data from publicly available sources without being directly involved in creating the data. This could be printed material but more commonly nowadays is online using your computer, hence the term 'desktop' research.

Desktop research is a quick, easy and cost-effective way to gather background information, insights and data relevant to a particular topic or research area. You can very easily and quickly gather existing knowledge, analyse data and draw your own conclusions on a wide range of information. This information includes market trends, competitor analysis, industry reports, customer preferences, case studies, academic studies and statistical data. However, it's **important to evaluate the credibility and reliability of the sources** used during desktop research to ensure the accuracy and validity of the information. Indeed, there are significant dangers involved with assuming everything on a website is the truth. Professional embarrassment is one risk, but making decisions based on poor data can have consequences that are much worse.

In the context of this book, we are focused on the items discussed in Chapter 4 in relation to understanding client priorities, developing a win strategy and mapping and aligning to the key stakeholders. There are many sources to consider and they usually start with an open internet search. Personally, I find it useful to start with **market and industry reports** that relate specifically to the organization you are working on; these can include industry journals and white papers. It's also useful to start with more of an 'independent' perspective, and sources could include research firms such as Gartner or Forrester as well as any of the many consulting/strategy/advisery organizations such as Deloitte, PricewaterhouseCoopers, KPMG, McKinsey or numerous others (big and small) that are available. But please be sure to check the reputation of those names that are not familiar to you.

You will often find market data referenced in these types of reports and you can go a step further to delve into the source data by visiting **online databases**. These include government datasets where you will find current and historical data trends for the industry you are researching. I'd also include **academic articles** here too, which can be found through searches on Google Scholar. As I can attest from my doctorate, they are very often hard to consume but packed with solid data and honest independent insight. Again, please check the validity as there is some dubious content published; a good test is to check the number of citations for a particular article.

Once you have this foundational perspective the rich organization-specific information will come from **organization websites**. These will offer valuable information about the way they want to present themselves, their strategy, products, services, organizational structure and financial performance. Here you will also find their **annual reports** (which can be a goldmine of information) and investor presentations. With specific detail about their goals, achievements and future plans they can also include letters from the chairman of the board, the CEO and often other key C-suite executives. You may also find **press releases** on the website and while it varies between organizations as to how often these are published, they are usually very insightful and useful items to consider. This is because they highlight the significant events chosen to be promoted. There are other types of insight that can be found in places such as **business media websites,** job advertisements, Glassdoor, consumer groups and trade associations. Checking **news reports** is also a great way to get a more independent view on the organization, and these can easily be sorted via the tabs when using an online search engine such as Google. The final source is **social media** which includes LinkedIn, X (formerly Twitter) and YouTube, among others.

Some of these will be discussed in more detail later in the chapter when we walk through how they should be used in the context of stakeholder research. It's also worth noting that at the time of writing this book it was the advent of ChatGPT, which is such a powerful tool to synthesize secondary data and help present it in a contextualized way. This will bring all of the above sources together and streamline the process as well as providing a much more comprehensive view.

Primary research through intelligence gathering

As noted earlier, the intelligence-gathering element to this step is primary research. It refers to the process of gathering firsthand information directly from relevant sources, that is, collecting data or insights directly from people who have the knowledge or experience. This method of research allows you to gather unique and specific information that either may not be available through other means or would be very difficult to find. Such information can be gathered through surveys or questionnaires, interviews in various forms, simply observing behaviours in short form or longer studies such as a case study, by conducting experiments/tests or by analysing existing information.

There are many forms of primary research but in the context of this book the methods to gather data would likely be observations and interviews. Let us start with **observations.** If you are fortunate enough to be 'walking the corridors' of a client organization and tune in your senses, you will pick up a huge amount of primary data. Things like **organizational culture** can be picked up from the office layout, how the common areas are organized, how people's desks are personalized (or not) and from different initiatives or activities on the notice boards. You can get a good view of the **employee dynamics** too; the diversity and working hours and style, such as whether they are eating lunch at their desk or together in the canteen, and you will certainly get a sense of morale. These observations will help you to understand their work culture, priorities and organizational values. The digital equivalent would be planning virtual 'coffee catch-ups' or other types of informal conversations with people on the client side. You may also get a sense of the culture and the different things being planned from employees' social media posts.

While observations will yield great insight, the biggest opportunity for primary research is with **interviews**. The word interview sounds more formal that it is, but I believe it does no harm to think about these interactions as interviews. You are collecting information, so take notes or do your best to remember the key details! There are many sources for interview data, but the easiest place to start is **internally** within your own organization.

Talk to people who have worked with or for the organization or person you are interested in. Next could be the **partner ecosystem**; talk to them to get an organizational-level and industry perspective. Perhaps you know **industry experts** and consultants who can give you their view on the state of the market, what the client values and any challenges they may be facing. You also have your **personal network** to flex for insight and intelligence as well as the **client organization** where you can talk to people at all levels. Putting this into action will be discussed later in the chapter when we detail the what and the how for stakeholder intelligence gathering, but be sure to have some structure to these conversations. To do this you need to prepare well to give you some key items that you would like to explore.

How desktop research and intelligence gathering work together

This step in the process explains how to gather the insights that will deliver success. Whether it's with key deals, key projects or key accounts, your success will be based on the quality of your information. As mentioned earlier, desktop research comes first and the intelligence gathering follows, and then the cycle tends to get repeated. Starting with the desktop research gives you the opportunity to get to grips with basic foundational knowledge – enough to be able to have a sensible and informed conversation and enough to be able to ask intelligent questions when you start your intelligence gathering.

While the desktop research side is imperative to provide the grounding, it's the information gleaned from conversations that provide the pearls of wisdom. This is because you will often get unique insights with greater depth and with real-time context, sometimes picking up things you were not aware of or expecting. This allows you to validate your thinking and test different ideas, all with the intention of creating something tailored and unique for your client.

Picking up from some of the identified items that are important to research and gather intelligence about, below I explain how intelligence gathering can supplement the desktop research, showcasing how the two do actually go hand-in-hand. These are grouped together under client priorities, developing a strategy for success and relationship strategy/mapping stakeholders. I also assign a value to each aspect which will be low, medium or high.

Client priorities

Identifying industry and market trends

- Desktop research provides a base level of knowledge, enough to be able to have an intelligent conversation. This is of medium value and you will need more in-depth insight, but it is crucial to do it before primary research so that you understand the context of the responses.
- Intelligence gathering through talking to people will help to identify the specific trends that clients are betting on and are most excited about. It is, therefore, of high value.

Identifying client priorities, interests and motivations

- Desktop research such as an interview with the CEO on YouTube or content from an annual report can form the basis for your key conversations. This is of medium value.
- Nothing beats hearing from clients and their direct reports about what specifically is important to them. This type of intelligence gathering is of high value.

Understanding organizational culture

- Organizational messages about culture will be on a company's website (desktop research), but public statements about company values can be similar. It is worth knowing but of relatively low value.

- What you learn from 'walking the corridors', having sidebar coffee chats and the virtual equivalents, will give you a much more powerful insight into the actual culture of a company (intelligence gathering). This is of high value.

Developing a strategy for success

Anticipating objections and concerns

- It will be quite hard to find objections and concerns from desktop research, other than those that might be generic. These include price, proof of technical performance and service-level agreement compliance. The value of desktop research is low, but it is worth preparing for generic objections.
- Having private conversations and posing the right questions to your key supporters and other stakeholders will help uncover their specific objections and concerns. This means the value of intelligence gathering is high.

Mitigating risks

- Through desktop research you can find key details such as their financial performance, merger and acquisition activities, key people changes and other significant corporate actions. This is of high value.
- You can use the understanding you gain from your desktop research to build credibility with the key stakeholders and dig deeper to uncover and validate any risks to the deal (intelligence gathering). Perhaps more importantly, you need to evaluate how the client perceives the risks inherent in your proposal. This insight is very high value.

Tailoring value proposition

- Understanding how you will deliver value to the client is the key to success for any deal, project or account. A lot can be gathered from desktop research to enable you to express your value proposition in terms that will appeal to the client. Therefore, this is of high value.
- Digging deeper through conversations with the client (intelligence gathering) will enable you to tailor the value proposition to their specific requirements and their KPIs, at an organizational, department and individual level. This is very high value.

Defining strategy for success

- You and your internal team will bring a point of view on your strategy to win with some inputs gleaned from desktop research, such as aligning to the published priorities of the C-suite, e.g. gathered from annual reports and interviews. The value of such information can be considered to be medium.

- To give your strategy the best chance of success you need the next level of detail. Discussions with key stakeholders are needed to validate and prioritize the core elements of your win strategy. This insight is very high value.

Competitive intelligence

- There will be some information about the competitor landscape in press releases, industry and business media databases or other such sources. The value of such desktop research is medium.
- The specifics on the direct competition – including their strengths and weaknesses as well as who is supporting them – will only come from good-quality intelligence gathering. As such, it's of high value.

Decision-making timelines and process

- Aside from linking budget cycles to year-end dates in organizational reports, it's unlikely that very much desktop research will be found on this aspect. Therefore, its value is likely to be low.
- The detail that is contextualized to the organization will come directly from intelligence gathering from the key stakeholders, so this is of high value.

Defining negotiation strategy

- There is relatively little desk research that could help here, but some high-level inferences about personality and style might be made from watching videos of the client's chief negotiator. Overall, the value of desk research for this category is low.
- As you are talking to key stakeholders and working through the details of the deal, project or account you will build a strong point of view as to how to position yourselves from a negotiation standpoint. So, this intelligence gathering is of high value.

Relationship strategy/mapping stakeholders

Understanding organizational structure

- A solid base can be created from published org charts, which means that such desktop research can be considered to be of medium value.

- The next level of detail will only come from intelligence gathering, such as understanding to whom key departments and people report. This would also include the informal lines of communication, any allegiances and any internal politics. Thus, its value is high. This insight can be fed back into Step 1, identifying stakeholders, as these interviews may reveal who the 'shapers' are in departments, the opinion leaders without formal power.

Identifying decision makers

- Using LinkedIn to identify stakeholders and layering that into the published material does provide a great base, certainly enough for you to have an intelligent conversation to validate further. This desktop research is considered to be high value.
- The nuances around who matters and their role will only come from intelligence gathering. Such depth is required to ensure you are aligning to the right people; consequently, it's of high value.

Understanding stakeholder priorities

- Depending how senior they are and how much they publish online, you can get a good base knowledge about stakeholders and their priorities from desktop research. Such knowledge is of medium value.
- Use the base knowledge you have generated to have an intelligent conversation with the stakeholders and dig deeper into the detail to refine and confirm your points. This intelligence gathering will be of high value.

Tailoring communication styles

- Desktop research may help you to understand preferred communication styles. For example, you can get a glimpse into a stakeholder's personality from watching videos of them, but these are not always available. Therefore, the overall value of this can be considered to be medium.
- You really need to do some intelligence gathering to supplement your insight. Getting coaching and support from the direct reports of the stakeholders will be the key to a smooth interaction with them. This is of high value.

The theme from above is that the real depth of insight, the things that will help you the most, actually come from the intelligence-gathering phase. However, desktop research provides a useful base from which to tailor the intelligence gathering.

Step 2a: Desktop research – social media channels

This section will present the main sources that can be used to gain insight into stakeholders and will be specifically at the stakeholder level rather than the broader organizational level. It will help you to set up a process to gather basic information that is publicly available, and there are a number of key items that I collect and places I go to get information that will be discussed in turn. How this can be captured and presented will be summarized at the end of this chapter.

Time at the organization and time in role

This information provides valuable insight into how influential the stakeholder can be. It takes a lot of time and energy to make things happen in a large organization, so knowing how familiar they are with the culture, the processes and how decisions are made is very important. This is because it's their internal network, and the levels of the trust and credibility they have built over their tenure will help to make things happen.

Let's consider three different scenarios when it comes to tenure, both with the organization and within the role, with each having its pros and cons. The first option is that they have been at the organization a long time and in their role a long time. The pros of this option are that these people will have in-depth knowledge of the organization, will have existing relationships and likely have a good level of credibility. In addition, they'll either have decision-making authority or know the back-channel process to get things done, and as they have been in the role a while there is an element of stability. In relation to the cons, they might be resistant to change and will almost certainly be very busy with their day-to-day activities, so getting their time and attention will be difficult.

The second option is someone who has been at the organization a long time but is new to their role, for example, they have recently been promoted. They'll have the same pros in the sense of organizational knowledge and existing relationships but will also have a fresh perspective on the role and its challenges. In addition, they'll want to prove they can deliver value quickly and have an impact, and to do that will likely be open to new ideas. On the cons side there is a learning curve and perhaps an aversion to taking big risks early on in the role.

The third option is someone who is both new to the organization and new to the role. In terms of the pros, these people will have the same enthusiasm for making an impact and have fresh thinking, and they will probably have a bit more time available to take in new ideas. However, the cons are that they'll lack internal relationships, influence and knowledge of the organizational culture and internal processes. Nonetheless, coming back to the pros, one strong plus point comes if you have worked with this person and delivered value in one of their previous roles. In that scenario my research shows that they'll likely be happy to have a conversation with you to do the same again. This is one of the best new business leads you can get.

LinkedIn profile and recent activity on LinkedIn

I'm old enough to remember doing my job before LinkedIn existed. The way I remember finding the names of the stakeholders who were important to my business was through trade and industry publications. I'd be in the office reading various newspapers and magazines and would cut out articles that mentioned key people. Then, I'd call the switchboard of the organization and ask to speak to the person. Funnily enough, as I'm thinking about that now, when compared to today it was actually a much more effective way of getting through to someone. This is because, more often than not, I'd get to speak to that person whereas today it seems almost impossible to get to someone senior using the same method.

The ineffectiveness of current methods places even more emphasis on leveraging existing relationships for intelligence gathering and introductions to other stakeholders. Nevertheless, LinkedIn is a fantastic tool which has changed the way we are able to identify stakeholders and how we can build and maintain relationships. However, it's worth noting that while there are currently (as of 2024) nearly a billion users on LinkedIn not everyone is on it and certainly not everyone will be an active user.

> Make sure your LinkedIn profile is as good as it can be since prospective clients and old contacts will be checking you out too. There is a lot of online material to help you with this, so review it and put it into action.

By exploring a stakeholder's profile, you are able to discover a wealth of information to identify shared experiences, their skills, areas of expertise or other insights that can help build rapport and establish common ground. At the time of writing this book, the profile was broken down into 10 sections: profile summary, highlights, featured, activity, about, experiences, education, skills, recommendations and interests. Each of these are briefly outlined next.

PROFILE SUMMARY

This section provides the basics such as their photo, organizational name, job title and geographical location. This can be useful for positioning where they fit within their organization and almost all profiles have a photo so you can actually see what the person looks like. The way someone looks has no impact on business but putting a face to a name is helpful. It forms part of the relationship-building process. Indeed, before our workplaces become so digital the majority of relationships started with a face-to-face meeting, and recognizing contacts is important.

HIGHLIGHTS

This section picks out anything that you have in common, such as if you have the same contacts or worked at the same organization. These are served up to you by LinkedIn as a catalyst for any common ground you might have.

FEATURED

A section where the user can choose to showcase anything in particular and requires the person to add content so that those visiting the profile are presented with this content. So, you can assume that this person wants you to see this, and it tends to be things they are particularly proud of or that define them and their role. Look out for videos of them here, as I find video always give me a better perspective into their personality and business style.

ACTIVITY

This is everything the person has posted on LinkedIn themselves as well as things they have 'liked', commented on or shared. So, this section provides a clear picture of what they care about and what they are promoting to the world. Taking some time here to review what people have posted and inter-acted with will yield a lot of insight. Even if you have to scroll back a while you might find personal things they have been part of, such as charity walks for certain causes or other activities that will give a window into their life beyond just the work side. Or sometimes you won't find anything, which would suggest they are not particularly active on the platform. Do bear in mind that the posts may have been written and even published by an exter-nal public relationship team.

ABOUT

This section requires the user to input content about themselves and tends to be content that describes their background and their journey to their current role. It can be a treasure trove of information and you will often find real nuggets of information here. However, in relation to people who rarely use LinkedIn it can be a bit outdated.

EXPERIENCES

This is the key section that most people use LinkedIn for and is where your current role as well as your past roles are listed in chronological order. Look out for the locations to see where they have been based, their previous job titles and most importantly the description of the role. Again, not everyone spends time on the description part, but it's still worth exploring to see what you can find.

EDUCATION

This list can go as far back as their time at university or may even include their school. Users can also add in here any of their professional qualifications. Again, this can be useful to see where they have been based, especially if they include the school days, as you could find out what city they were born in to try to find some common ties or parallels. The same goes for their university days. It's all about exploring areas where you may have an affinity that is essentially outside of work but forms part of the journey to where they are now, workwise. However, be careful about taking this too far as some decision makers might be uncomfortable with ice-breakers about their hobbies or hometown. You aren't doing anything wrong by accessing this publicly available information, but use it with caution.

SKILLS

This section comes from your connections' endorsements and enables you to get a sense of what others think this person is good at. For this reason it can be a useful sense check as to their role. For example, if a lot of people have endorsed the person for 'project management' versus 'product design', you will be able to place them better. Again, be cautious as their roles can change. I remember LinkedIn asking me a lot for these in the past (for other people) but not much lately, so I don't think it's as widely promoted as it once was.

RECOMMENDATIONS

This section gives you a feel for the qualities that people perceive this person has. These will be a mixture of the person asking for a recommendation and people proactively writing a recommendation. You will get a real sense of people's opinion of this person using their own words and will get an insight into their management style and personality.

INTERESTS

This section lists the people, groups and associations that this person follows and will give a flavour of which individuals they are interested in. This could give an insight into their cultural or political leanings, giving you a sense of potential 'hot button' subjects to avoid. Perhaps they follow your company or even a competitor, but whoever they follow will tell you something about them, even if just a glimpse.

So, the idea with a LinkedIn profile review is to dig deeper into their professional background and to take in this information to build a holistic picture in your mind of who this person is, where are they from and what they care about.

Their X profile

A stakeholder's X profile can provide additional perspectives and insights into their professional – and more importantly – their personal interests, opinions and industry engagement. By understanding their presence on this platform you can identify topics they find important, follow their conversations and engage in meaningful interactions. Such knowledge can be leveraged to build rapport, demonstrate industry knowledge and align your value proposition with their interests. This service tends to be more about what they are currently interested in and not about their past, although you can scroll back to see the entire history. Regular users will also often mention where they are in the world and if they are travelling or attending events. This is useful and interesting information as it stands but can also form part of a conversation starter for when you meet them (whether in person or via virtual meetings).

> Based on what people are posting and its relevance to you and your business, there is the opportunity to engage with this content. In fact, there is a business development and prospecting strategy called 'social selling' that actively

encourages this as a way to start the relationship-building process. I'm not delving into this approach within this book, but I would say that if it makes sense for you to comment or engage in a post or tweet then by all means do so. However, I'd caution against overdoing it.

Anything posted on YouTube

A stakeholder's presence on YouTube (or other video content on X or LinkedIn) can provide additional information about their areas of expertise, thought leadership or public speaking engagements. By reviewing their videos or online content we can gain insights into their communication style, personality, interests and perspectives. As video, it's a lot easier to interpret the content to tailor your communication and presentation approaches so it will resonate with them. This will help make sure that your interactions are memorable and engaging. I always take the time to try to identify anything on YouTube as I find it to be of huge value; it could be a video from a speaking engagement a few years ago or a more recent corporate video on a particular subject or event. I find these can also be good talking points to mention when you meet, e.g. 'I was doing some research and I saw your video on YouTube about xyz, I wanted to ask you abc ...'.

Step 2b: Desktop research – other public sources

Searching for a published biography or other type of personal profile

Examining a stakeholder's published biography or profile (usually on their current organization's website) provides another input into building a picture of an individual's background. Notably, these are more common when the person is a senior executive. A lot of the key milestones will be covered within the LinkedIn profile but often you will get a bit more depth and a more nuanced view of how they want their career to be perceived from their biography. So, it's definitely worthwhile trying to find these and reading them through for extra insight.

Speaking engagement at industry events

If the stakeholder is speaking at events this can offer an insight into their industry involvement and interests. It will also help to understand the topics they find relevant, the communities they engage with and the influencers they associate with. For example, if a stakeholder has spoken at events or participated in panel discussions on topics such as data privacy and security, it indicates their emphasis on these areas. These might be promoted by themselves via the platforms already discussed, but they can usually also be found by doing an open internet search. Depending on where these events are and how big they are there might also be the opportunity to attend and try to meet them in person. At the very least the event could be a talking point should you ever meet, especially if you were there in person.

Published articles and news reports

Reviewing published articles and any news items about the stakeholder or their organization can provide valuable context and background information. It can reveal their industry prominence based on the sheer number of articles. It can also provide an insight into their public image and reputation which can assist in building rapport, and any news articles may also highlight their challenges or business priorities. It's easy to do an open internet search and filter by 'news' to see if you get any hits, and large organizations will have research teams that support this process.

Notes

I'll mention more at the end of this chapter on how to capture this insight, but keeping with the Microsoft Excel format I suggest using a column at the end of the file to capture notes or anything that is of particular interest to you or the team. This can act as a summary of the key items discovered through the research as well as other talking points that are important to capture.

LinkedIn Sales Navigator allows you to save accounts and people (they are called 'leads') and will serve up details of posts or where they are in the news into one cockpit-style dashboard. It doesn't cover everything we discussed here but is a good place to start.

Intelligence gathering in the context of the three use cases

We finished the last section with the first two elements of Step 2, which were linked to desktop research. Before we discuss the final three elements, which are linked to intelligence gathering, it is important to set some context. Gathering a good foundational perspective on each of the stakeholders from the desktop research needs to be done first as this helps with your credibility when you begin talking to them directly as part of the intelligence-gathering phase. When we do gather intelligence, it tends to come from two perspectives, that of organizational level and stakeholder level.

Organizational level: among other things you can gain insight into their corporate priorities and pain points, the competitor landscape (which includes their perceived strengths and weaknesses), organizational structure and operations, their work culture and a high-level view of the decision-making processes.

Stakeholder level: getting insight on the individual stakeholders and their unit-level priorities and pain points, how they are aligned internally within the organization, any personal allegiances to competitors and insight into their management and personality style.

At this step in the process it's important to note that we are simply collating information on those stakeholders identified in Step 1 who might be able to help us with some insight and intelligence. We are not reaching out to them as part of this step, and this will be covered in Chapter 6 which details Step 3 about the relationship engagement strategy. Before we go into the final three elements of Step 2, let's think about the intelligence-gathering sources to which you have access.

Sources for intelligence gathering

I've broken down the sources into two broad groups. The first is your personal network and the second is the network of your organization, noting that there may be some overlap between the two. This section will be leveraging the total sum of the relationship capital that exists across these two groups; that is everyone you know and everyone your organization knows.

The easiest way to keep track of your and your colleagues' personal connections is by using LinkedIn. As already mentioned, LinkedIn has been a game changer on so many levels and will be referenced throughout this section on intelligence gathering. I'm not going to explain in any depth how to set up the LinkedIn searches since there are many online tutorials which can be found that will explain the 'how' part in detail, but suffice to say that it is very user friendly and intuitive.

From a LinkedIn perspective your personal network is made up of your 1st-degree connections. This should be who you personally know, but anyone that uses LinkedIn a lot (and has a lot of connections) will know that not all of these connections are solid personal relationships. Indeed, I'd suggest that the vast majority are not actually personal relationships; however, we need to start somewhere. Leveraging the 1st-degree connections that exist within your and your organization's network will help you gather intelligence about key deals, key projects and key accounts.

There is also the concept of 2nd-degree connections. Such connections are made through 1st-degree connections who know someone else that you would like to build a relationship with within the target client organization.

As we discuss the two different ways to gather intelligence it will become apparent that a lot of effort is required to sift through the data to find relationships that could potentially help you. I call it the 'panning for gold' stage. Going through the 1st- and in particular the 2nd-degree connections that exist will be a tedious and time-consuming process. How much time you are able to devote to this is dependent on the significance and importance of the deal, project or account. However, too many times I've seen how relationships can be the difference between success and failure, so in my humble opinion it is always worth taking this extra time to try to uncover that nugget of gold that can make the difference.

Your personal network

The value of your relationship capital has been discussed a lot so far in this book, in particular in Chapter 1. As outlined above, in the context of LinkedIn these are your 1st-degree connections. It's worthwhile doing a relationship audit and trying to add as many people from your past as you can. I'd recommend thinking about the people you knew before you were active on LinkedIn, maybe from school, college or university and tracking them down and adding them to your network. This might also prompt an opportunity to have a long overdue catch-up with an old friend!

Also, as a matter of course when you build a new relationship with someone, in particular if you meet them in person or on a virtual meeting, it's imperative that you always add those people on LinkedIn. Worst-case scenario, if not accepted you can automatically 'follow' them now which allows you to capture that relationship for situations like this. You will find that the bigger your network the greater the chance you will find people who can help you.

The collective network of your organization

If you are working on a key deal, project or account the impact of leveraging the relationship capital that exists across your own organization will transform the way you operate. When you think about it, of all the groups of people that can help you with this type of intelligence it's those working within your own organization who tend to have a vested interest in helping you, as you are on the same mission. And when people do help you it can be a good idea to give them some recognition, public or otherwise.

If you want to leverage the collective network of your organization the first thing to do is to connect with as many people as possible within it. To identify the gaps, you can start by setting up a search within LinkedIn to see how many of your organization's employees are on it. At the time of writing this book, the process is simply to go to the LinkedIn homepage and search for your organization. Next, click 'people', then the 'current company' drop-down tab where you can insert your organization's name into the text box. This will show the total number. From there you can filter to see how many 1st-degree connections you have and compare this to the total number.

Depending on the size of your organization it might not be practical to connect with everyone, but I'd suggest connecting with as many as possible; certainly, the key management and top executives in key regions and verticals. To give you a sense of proportion, I currently work for a smaller organization which at the time of writing had 234 people on LinkedIn. For this organization I can expect to connect with almost everyone, but I previously worked for one that has over 200,000 people on LinkedIn. This would clearly be more complicated to connect with everyone, so I needed to choose the right ones wisely! You will generally notice that people at the same organization are very willing to connect with one another. Once you are connected to as many as possible you can get insight into their relationships, not to mention that when some of them leave (e.g. to a client organization) you have this existing relationship to tap into later!

When adding organizations into LinkedIn, always add as many of the different entities as you can. Sometimes, LinkedIn will show the main organization but also list the consulting arm or the digital arm as separate entities. In such instances it is best to click them all when doing the search.

There are three routes to explore when gathering intelligence and ideally you should follow them in sequence, but it doesn't always work out like that. The point is to try to talk to the key stakeholder within the client organization once you have gathered a base level of intelligence (this is in addition to your desktop research), as then you will likely have more context.

Step 2c: Intelligence gathering – used to work at target organization

Identifying those who used to work at the target organization (the target) and now work elsewhere is a great first step into intelligence gathering. Since they no longer work at the organization you are interested in, they are more likely to be open and honest and potentially more likely to give you information that they might previously have felt uncomfortable about sharing. This information can include negative things as well as the names of the key people (and what they are really like); however, be careful as this can throw up a huge number of datapoints and it can take a lot of time to sift through it all.

One thing to watch out for is how long ago they left; for example, if it was over 12 months ago then the information becomes less valuable since it may be outdated. This is a very simple search that can be created on LinkedIn or Sales Navigator where you set 'past company' as the target. There are a number of ways to search, four of which will be discussed next.

They used to work at the target and now work at your organization

This is a great one that I usually do first, and a search can uncover immensely powerful relationships. Having already set past company to the target, now set 'current company' to your organization. Now you have a list of all the people that used to work at your target, and because they now work for your organization their allegiances now lie there. These people can become huge allies both for intelligence and also potentially as part of the deal, project or account team. What can they share? Do they know the stakeholders? Do they know people that know the stakeholders? Can they make introductions to others who currently work at their previous organization?

Your 1st-degree connections

Once you have the search set up to show the 'previous company' as the target, you can then click on the filter to only show your 1st-degree connections. This will identify those you have a direct connection with and will require you to scan through each contact to make a sense check as to whether you think they could help you. Each of them will have previously worked at your target and you therefore have to think about whether they'd be willing to help you based on the quality of your relationship and/or their openness to help someone with this type of request.

TeamLink connections

Picking up on the value of leveraging your internal network, there is an easy way to uncover relationships that your organization has, but it does need to hold LinkedIn Sales Navigator licences. If you have these licences there is a feature called 'TeamLink' that allows you to automatically see all the relationships, whether you are connected to them or not. However, this will only work for those who have a Sales Navigator licence and not every employee will be given one. As a result there will be some gaps between who has a Sales Navigator licence and the total number of employees, but these gaps can be plugged with the point above regarding connecting to as many people as possible. One of the benefits of TeamLink is that you can zoom in on only the relationships involving your organization without having to sift through all the 1st-degree connections to find only colleagues.

Your 2nd-degree connections

I've listed this one here only to say that depending on the size of your network and the size of the target, it's probably going to throw up way too many results for you to be able to manage. Consequently, it would be unlikely to be a good option here.

Pros and cons of Step 2c

Pros: these people will provide you with an external perspective from those who have worked within the client organization, and they'll likely provide very candid and valid insights into the client's operations, strategies, competition and organizational structure.

Cons: depending on how long ago they worked there the information could be outdated. Also, perspectives may differ from one former employee to the next, and their experiences may not be a fair representation of the current state of the client organization.

> This route demands the most amount of effort with potentially the least amount of insight. So, depending on how much time you have and how important this deal, project or account is, there is a risk-reward ratio to consider. At the very least, it will be worthwhile reviewing the search results to see if anyone jumps out and is worthy of further investigation.

Step 2d: Intelligence gathering – partners and other external relationships

This one is more from your organization's perspective than your personal relationship network. So, you need to get a good understanding of who your organization has in its partner ecosystem, and this includes all the organizations that your organization works with. This can be integration partners and go-to-market partners or even suppliers or other clients. If these partners have an existing relationship with the target it can offer you valuable insights into the client's business objectives, priorities and decision-making processes. Through conversations with them you can gather this information about the client as well as get an insight into the competitor landscape. In an ideal situation you will be strategically aligned with this partner and, if so, you then can leverage that relationship to bring you extra credibility in the client's eyes. There are a number of options to explore to gather partner ecosystem information, three of which are discussed next.

Talk to people internally

If you have a partner, alliances or adviser relationships team, these are the first place to go. They are a great resource and one that I often see underleveraged.

This is because when talking to most colleagues you are essentially asking them to do you a favour. However, when you ask the partner, alliances or adviser relationships team for help it's actually their job to do this, so they want to make these connections to power your organization forward! At this stage you want to create a master list at an organizational level of all the partners and advisers (or others) that your organization has relationships with. Next, spend time talking to this team to determine who they know within each of the organizations; for example, it can help you if they have deep relationships with the leadership or regional executives. At the very least, if you give them a brief they'll be able to do some digging around on your behalf to see what they can find out as well as who they can introduce you to. Go through the same exercise with others to gather inputs for the master list.

Software such as Introhive

This will provide you with a comprehensive view of all the relationships that currently exist within your organization at a specific partner or adviser level. You can then talk to the person holding that relationship internally to see if they can help you with an introduction. This saves a lot of time and effort and gets you straight to the right people.

LinkedIn search

At the time of writing it is not possible to create a filter on LinkedIn that would allow you to search your connections to only show people who 1) currently work for a partner and 2) have existing relationships with your target. What you need to do is to search your 1st-degree connections to see if you know anyone currently working in one of the partners or advisers that you believe can help you with your target, and then reach out to them via the partner team to see if they can assist.

Pros and cons of Step 2d

Pros: as the partner is a supplier too, and likely in a similar or adjacent industry (assuming this as you are partners), they'll give you very contextualized insight into the buying and approval process. They'll also share specifics about how the target is to work with.

Cons: the success of this process is dependent on the strength of your organization's relationship with the partner as well as on the partner's ability to get the right people to the table on their side. Partners can understandably be hesitant to share sensitive information and there might be competing priorities, so gathering intelligence from partners can prove difficult, but when it works it usually works very well.

Step 2e: Intelligence gathering – currently works at the target organization

This route is where the most insight can be gained and, thus, where the most effort goes. Getting a full view on all the relationships you and your organization have within your target will be crucial to your success. These conversations will provide valuable insights into the organization's culture, decision-making dynamics, competitive landscape and potential road-blocks. They can therefore help you understand the client's internal challenges, political landscape and any competing priorities that might impact the deal. There are a number of ways to do this, as will be discussed next.

Used to work at your organization, now works at the target (alumni)

This is one search I'm always keen to see as these are people who know your organization and its value proposition. They can be a valuable asset, although they'll understandably be unwilling to share too much sensitive information. Make sure you engage through the best route based on who has the best relationship as opposed to you just reaching out randomly. This will be explained more in Chapter 6. These people can be found through conducting a similar search on LinkedIn as before, with 'previous company' set to your organization and 'current company' to the target.

Internal detective work

This is an extension of the work that was done as part of Chapter 4 when you were developing the master list of relationships to identify all the existing stakeholders. It includes checking CRM and other systems and talking to the leadership to gather as much information as possible. Once you have this base data keep digging to make sure you get as complete a picture as you can.

Software such as Introhive

Using this type of software avoids utilizing tribal knowledge and undertaking detective work. This is because the software enables you to immediately see a full list of everyone at your organization who has a relationship within the target, although that is dependent on them communicating via their work email. You would also be able to see the strength of that relationship if they do communicate via email, as the software also enables you to see the frequency and number of interactions.

Your 1st-degree connections

As discussed in the 'used to work at target company' section, you set up the search in the same way but with the 'target company' being the 'current company'. These results will be your core universe of existing direct relationships within that organization, so take the time to go through each one and do the same sense check to see if their role means that they could be useful. Once you have done this you can then establish the best engagement strategy.

TeamLink connections

The TeamLink connections will be much more powerful here than in the scenario outlined in the first route because they'll showcase everyone internally who has a relationship with someone within your target. From using Introhive (or other similar software) you will have more detailed insight into the strength of the relationship, and this view will show those that have a 1st-degree connection.

Your 2nd-degree connections

This search will identify people that you are connected to as a 1st-degree connection, and these people will have a 1st-degree connection at the target. Depending on the size of your network and the size of the target this number can be quite big, so it's a judgement call as to how much time you put into it. Also, remember if you do not have Sales Navigator and if you have connected to as many of your current employees as possible, those people will show up here. So, you will need to keep a special eye out for those internal relationships as you sift through this data.

In my experience the most powerful relationships, and the ones that signify the difference between success and failure, are those with key people on the client side. Some call them the 'internal champion', others 'the fox'. These people will help you navigate within the client organization and can assist you with getting introductions, or they can do detective work themselves and help you that way. Without this ally (or allies) internally it can be very hard to be successful. However, you need to arm them with the correct and most relevant information as you are, in effect, responsible for enabling them to make things happen. Examples of this will be discussed within Part 3 (Chapters 7, 8 and 9).

Pros and cons of Step 2e

Pros: this is up-to-date information straight from the organization.

Cons: depending on where they sit in the organization their purview might not allow them to share the type of insight you are looking for, nor may they be open to sharing sensitive information.

Capturing and presenting this insight

There are two parts to capturing and presenting the insights gathered during the three-step process. First, capturing and recording the key details to be used by the core team for internal analysis and, second, how to present data to others internally, including management. The final chapter (Chapter 10) will discuss in more detail how you implement, end to end, the process that is outlined in this book. However, it's important to have an internal document to capture the key sources and details as you are working through these steps. You could capture this detail in its most rudimentary form in a Microsoft Excel or Google Sheets spreadsheet.

When just starting out, the simplest way to do this is to have one master sheet to capture the data for all three steps. Figure 4.2 showed the template structure you can use for Step 1. In the same style and format you can extend the columns along to capture any datapoints you find for the headings covered above, for both desktop research (e.g. time at company and in role, their LinkedIn profile plus other social media profiles and space for notes) and intelligence gathering (e.g. used to work at client, now works at your company etc). It is not practical to show an example in a figure here since there are too many columns.

As previously mentioned, I have ready-to-use templates with all the headings pre-populated, and I can share these with you at no cost. Please contact me at www.ryan-osullivan.com for these templates.

Building stakeholder profiles

In Step 1 we developed an initial list of key stakeholders on the deal, project or account, and through Step 2 we've walked through how to conduct desktop research and intelligence gathering on the key stakeholders. As you begin discussing this with an extended audience internally, it's very important to present the status in an effective and professional manner. We have the org chart from Step 1 to showcase where the key people sit and how this all fits together, and sitting behind each key stakeholder you can think about a profile. This can be any format that suits you, such as Microsoft PowerPoint or Word (or equivalent). These profiles will be used as part of Step 3, when you begin engaging with key stakeholders. Whether it's you personally, or more likely others within your organization, some context will be needed and the base content will come from Steps 1 and 2. So, this should be used to populate the profile along with any additional information that is collected from Step 3 and then repeating the whole process. I have sample templates for these which I can share if you contact me via www.ryan-osullivan.com.

What we've learned in this chapter

The key things we have learned in this chapter are the difference between primary and secondary data (and how they work together), and the five elements to Step 2 (research and intelligence gathering), which are:

- 2a: desktop research – social media channels.
- 2b: desktop research – other public sources.
- 2c: intelligence gathering – used to work at target organization.
- 2d: intelligence gathering – partners and other external relationships.
- 2e: intelligence gathering – currently works at prospect organization.

What's coming next

Next is the final step in the three-step process. This is creating and executing on a carefully orchestrated engagement strategy and it contains three elements:

- 3a: the importance of multi-threading.
- 3b: execution of the engagement strategy.
- 3c: shifting from org chart to relationship map.

6

How to build and execute a relationship map: Step 3, relationship engagement strategy

Introduction

CAROLINE MACKRILL, ACCENTURE – MANAGING DIRECTOR,
ADVISER RELATIONS LEAD, EUROPE

This chapter introduces the 'fun' part of the three-step process, the engagement strategy. In the previous chapters you have been doing the hard graft, the research and the planning. You have identified your contacts and done your analysis. In this chapter, you will now be putting all that hard work into practice and starting to engage with your targets. The planning prior to the execution is essential, as you have one shot at this and if you go in unprepared and without a clear objective you can blow it at the first interaction. The old adage of people buy from people is key here. Have you got the right personalities interacting with your target stakeholders? If this isn't a direct relationship of yours, do you have the right person making the introductions? One of the main pitfalls with an engagement strategy is when people say they have a relationship when they don't. You need to define 'know' before allowing someone to make the introduction. As the person planning the engagement, you need to own your strategy and be the conductor of the orchestra, ensuring that you have the right team paired to the right stakeholder.

In this chapter you are given a very clear guide as to what to do when. It is important though that any interactions do not come across as prescriptive. The planning is vital, but when you make that ultimate in-person contact those interactions must appear spontaneous and 'human'. Having the right content for each stakeholder is also key and if you can take something to them that they don't know, it could pique their interest. Notably, when engaging with potential clients they don't want to know all about you, they want to know what you can do to help them with a specific issue. In all interactions with your targets make them the hero of the piece and not you, and remember that the first five minutes and the last 10 minutes are critical. However engaging you are, if you are talking to a group of people their attention will naturally wander, so it is important to bring them back to the conversation with engaging statements like 'in summary'. This will bring them back into the room and ensure that your message is hitting the right spot.

There is a science to how you interact with potential clients, and the whole company should be leveraged to support the building of key stakeholder relationships. As well as internal action, you can use your existing clients to support the engagement and make introductions for you. This chapter explains in depth the importance of multi-threading in that there are many different routes to the execution of an effective engagement strategy. It shows the importance of planning, research and detailed analysis before any direct conversations take place. Get the 'behind the scenes' work done properly and you will find that engagement will be much easier and have a greater chance of success.

What is an engagement strategy?

What have we achieved so far with the first two steps of this relationship-mapping process? We have a basic understanding of the client's priorities; we are developing a strategy that we think will make us successful; we've identified an initial set of key stakeholders on the deal, project or account; and we are building a picture of who we know and who we don't know. In addition, we've done some desktop research across the organization and, in particular, on the identified key stakeholders, and have also spent time identifying those we believe may be able to help us with intelligence. So now what? Well now comes the most crucial part; so far all this work has been done in the background but now we need to start engaging with people.

An engagement strategy is a planned approach for effectively interacting and communicating with the defined key stakeholders and others we believe can help us. The engagement strategy outlines the methods, channels of communication and the activities that you – at individual and organizational level – will employ to achieve the specific goals. In this case these are winning key deals, making key projects successful and growing key accounts.

There are two objectives to this effort. First, to continue to gather intelligence and validate or supplement what was already known and what was found through desktop research about the organization and key stakeholders. Second, to engage with key stakeholders on the deal, project or account.

The more work you do on the intelligence gathering the better positioned you are for when you interact directly with key stakeholders. As we move through this chapter it will become apparent that when it comes to talking to people to gather intelligence, you are completely dependent on that person's willingness to help you. Why would this identified connection help you (or whoever the conduit is)? People are busier than ever, so what is in it for them? Are you providing value to them or are you asking for a favour?

Initially, and especially in the intelligence-gathering phase, it tends to be that you are asking for a favour. Consequently, I'd suggest that their willingness to help is primarily linked to the quality of the relationship they have with the person asking for help. What goodwill have they built up? What relationships capital exists? Or what potential value do they see in being owed a favour from the person asking for help?

I'd argue that there is an x and a y axis. On the x axis you have the strength of the relationship, while on the y axis you have the seniority or importance of the person asking the favour. There is no need to do this for real but if you imagine in your mind all the potential connections mapped on this scale, the top right of this quadrant would show strong relationships with a senior person asking for help. These would be the most valuable ones followed by strong relationships with less senior people asking and, finally, a senior person asking when they have a weaker relationship with the person they are asking.

Step 3a: The importance of multi-threading

With this in mind, a crucial part of your success with key deals, key projects and key accounts is your ability to multi-thread. This is the practice of establishing and nurturing multiple relationships within a client organiza-tion and among key stakeholders, but you can't hold all these relationships. So, multi-threading involves multiple people from your side engaging with various people on the client side across their different seniority levels, departments or functions, the aim being to build rapport, influence and support throughout the decision-making process. While the relationship map is managed centrally, multi-threading focuses on creating a network of relationships that are held by multiple individuals from your side.

Broadening your team helps you to cover the client account more effec-tively, and when you pair suitable people you will see the deal progress faster. This is because if one relationship encounters challenges, having multiple threads decreases the risk of the deal stalling. There will be an increased influence if multiple people on the client side are engaged.

A Gartner[19] study from 2022 found that the average deal has between 11 and 15 key decision makers, and that organizations practising multi-threading outperform competitors by 50 per cent.

You will need to maximize the power of your organization's network. Through the previous process of developing the list of who can help with intelligence gathering, you will have a broader idea of who you can bring into your team based on those that have some knowledge or existing rela-tionships within the target organization. However, there are others to consider too, and you will need to think about who you can leverage and what role they can play as part of your deal, project or account.

Once you acknowledge that you can't handle everyone, you will need to take a look at the key stakeholders with the intention of mapping different stakeholders with different people from your side. The idea is that these people become the relationship holder of that key stakeholder (or their direct report). As the relationship naturally develops between your organi-zation and the client there will be numerous interactions. These will likely be the opportunity for you to involve more people from your side in the physical or virtual meetings. These opportunities then become the occasion to try to multi-thread, and there are things you can do at different stages in the relationship.

Prior to meeting key stakeholders

You can discuss who will be paired with who prior to any meeting but try not to do too many pairings in one meeting. These pairings can be based on seniority, job function or geographical location as well as softer aspects such as personality or nationality. It's important to note that the person on the client side will usually respond better to someone they consider to be a peer, or where there is a sense of familiarity. Think back to Chapter 3 and the points on propinquity (people build relationships with people in their geographical proximity) and homophily (people build relationships with people who like the same things as them). Your work with the research and intelligence gathering will help you with key points about each person.

During initial meetings with key stakeholders

The person from your side will make a specific effort during the meeting to align themselves to their pairing on the client side, perhaps saying specific things during their introduction that might trigger a spark. Some things are obvious but also think outside of the box. For example, if you are having a meeting in the US or UK and have a Brazilian on your team, and one of the key stakeholders is also Brazilian, then this provides a 'readymade' connection that could be leveraged. Another example could be two people who live in the same town or went to the same university. The point is that these are all things to try to use as a catalyst to encourage a relationship to form; however, it usually can't be the only thing. There also needs to be something around matching job role and/or seniority, but these softer things can be the spark and can be used to your advantage.

   Once initially introduced, the person from your side can make a suggestion that would require sending something to their pairing or otherwise sharing something that they'd consider to be valuable to them, for example, a white paper, case study or article (professional or personal). However, make sure this doesn't come across as being too obvious, so try to test the temperature to make it seem natural.

After meeting key stakeholders

This is the key stage. After the meeting, your person sends a one-on-one message to their pairing with the promised content and tries to establish a separate relationship. Hopefully, they'll reply to thank you for doing this but if they don't, I'd suggest that you do nothing. Decision makers are busy people, and I certainly don't suggest following up with a 'just checking you got this' type of message. Just hold off until you need to get in touch for something else and when that happens, the last message they see will be the thread of you providing value to them – which is positive. The best scenario is they engage with you and want to talk more about the content or something else and if this happens, grab the opportunity with both hands. While these efforts involve engagement at an individual level, they should always be coordinated with the wider team and form part of the wider, agreed-upon strategy.

After you send a polite reply to their thank you it can be left almost dormant for now, and as the key deal, project or account progresses you have the option to leverage that one-to-one relationship. It could be something as simple as asking for a quick conversation (e.g. if an issue arises or saying you are in town or close to their office and inviting them to meet for a coffee). How they respond to these overtures, and indeed if they even respond, will also give you an indication as to how well placed you are on the deal, project or account. For example, if you are in a good position they'll be more willing to invest in the relationship, less likely to ignore you and more likely to want to spend time with you.

> Unfortunately, I've seen multi-threading done in clumsy and mechanical ways in the past and it fails, sometimes badly. An example of this would be when one of your C-suite executives tries to build a relationship with their peer on the client side, but the client doesn't engage. However, your C-suite executive continues to follow up. This can irritate the client and prompt complaints, so take care with who you ask to do this and be sensitive to how it can come across.

Leveraging your internal network

There are many groups across your organization that can be considered in this multi-threading exercise. The industry you are in will determine the specific role types, so I'll be broad in the groupings below and have removed all job titles within each grouping (other than referring to the broad C-suite).

YOUR C-SUITE AND EXECUTIVE TEAM

This group includes all of your organization's leadership – the C-suite and their direct reports as well as anyone else typically considered as part of the executive team. Involvement from these people in the deal signifies your organization's commitment and support, and this will instil confidence in key stakeholders about the importance of the deal, project or account.[20] These leaders can communicate the organization's strategic vision, demonstrating how the client aligns with the long-term objectives of the organization and fostering a sense of partnership at the executive level. Such relationships are crucial when issues inevitably arise, something which can happen on any deal, project or account.

SALES TEAMS/BUSINESS DEVELOPMENT/ACCOUNT MANAGEMENT/CLIENT PARTNERS

This group are the people responsible for selling, and could be what some might call the 'hunters', which is hunting to find completely new clients, i.e. selling that initial deal. On the other hand it could be the 'farmers', who are growing revenue from existing clients. These people tend to have a good view on the specific customer needs and pain points as well as different commercial insights. They can be brought in to offer a customer perspective, whether it's for the actual client you are working with or sharing what you have achieved with peers of theirs in the market. I would expect the majority of the readers of this book to come from this category.

PROJECT DELIVERY TEAMS

This includes everyone responsible for delivering the outcome for the client, whether it's services or a product being delivered. Bringing these people into the conversation can add real credibility as they are the ones actually doing the work and delivering the solution. Delivery leads can focus on their successful execution of projects, explaining how they ensured that deliverables met the client expectations and how quality is maintained, thereby instilling confidence in key stakeholders. From their experience they can discuss the risks and explain how these were addressed, for example, navigating the change process, addressing resistance and providing guidance to ensure a successful adoption of the solution.

SUBJECT MATTER EXPERTS/TECHNICAL EXPERTS/SOLUTION CONSULTANTS/ PRODUCT OWNERS/HORIZONTAL SALES TEAMS/SERVICE LINE LEADS/PRODUCT OWNERS/BUSINESS VALUE CONSULTANTS

These people have knowledge and experience in a very specific area. They could be subject matter or technical experts who know about a specific industry or have functional or technical expertise. They could also include solution consultants or product owners who are experts on your own organization's products. Then there are the horizontal and service line specialists who are experts on a specific service, product or solution.

The main contribution of such people is their in-depth knowledge about the organization's offerings, enabling them to address complex requirements and provide valuable insights to key stakeholders. They can analyse the client's needs and tailor solutions to meet specific requirements, thus ensuring alignment and demonstrating the value of the proposed solution. They can also establish themselves as thought leaders, sharing industry insights, trends and best practices with stakeholders to position the organization as a trusted adviser. These resources are often scarce, so you will need to navigate your organization effectively and build the right internal relationships.

LEGAL/INFORMATION SECURITY/GOVERNANCE/DATA PRIVACY TEAMS

These people tend to represent the parts of the organization that can be the root of any potential obstacles. Often, clients might be concerned with their internal policies with regard to risk appetite, data privacy policies and their information security protocols. In these scenarios it could be reassuring to have your experts talk through the approach and try to ease their concerns through dialogue. Once you are further along in the process it's always best for these teams to talk to each other rather than you trying to be the go-between. This isn't so much about multi-threading; its purpose is more to reduce the time it takes to get to an agreement and to avoid confusion.

OTHER INTERNAL FUNCTIONS

This includes your marketing, finance, purchasing, HR and all other internal functions that exist within your organization. These people are great to leverage as they have a huge amount of credibility. Think about the personas you are interacting with on the client side, whether it's marketing or HR people or perhaps sales enablement. Whoever it is, if you have someone internally who can talk to clients about how they are solving the issues that the client has, this can be golden. They are peers and may know the same people or go to the same events, and because they are somewhat removed from the deal, project or account the client will likely be more relaxed and open during any conversation.

Leveraging your external network

EXISTING CLIENTS

One of the best ways for you to multi-thread is by introducing your client to another existing client. This can be done as part of a joint meeting over lunch or perhaps coffee, but it's most effective when they are left to talk in private, either over the phone or in person. Clearly, large parts of what happens during those private conversations will remain private, but the impact of these conversations can be very strong.

By the very virtue of who they are talking to (let's assume it's a senior person at a reputable organization), this reflects well on you and your organization, thereby building credibility and trust. It demonstrates that you have a track record of successful relationships and projects. This can instil confidence in the client and make them more comfortable. They'll also get an insight into how well you collaborate together, how you solve problems and mitigate risks, the general quality of the overall output and what it's like to work with you long term. So, think carefully about who would be good to pair together.

PARTNER ECOSYSTEM

I've already talked about identifying and leveraging the relationships that exist within your partner ecosystem, and this is an extension of that. The ideal scenario is that a partner both you and your client work with communicates a positive message about you within the client organization. This is especially valuable if your solutions – and those of the partner – are connected to or work alongside one another. You can benefit from the trust your partners have built from their successful track record and their ability to deliver results. Their expertise and specialization in specific areas can enhance the perception of your organization's capabilities. The partners could share case studies and success stories of how you have worked well together, further reinforcing the client's confidence in you and your solution.

INDUSTRY ADVISERS AND INDEPENDENT EXPERTS

This group was also covered earlier when referring to existing relationships within the partner, alliance and adviser ecosystem; however, I've separated it out here as the adviser and independent experts have far-reaching impacts beyond existing relationships. As such, there are research companies that publish data and reports on the key players in specific industries and domains. These reports are 'independent' so should not be influenced by your organization, and that is why they try to create an arm's-length relationship with the organizations they evaluate.

However, that doesn't mean that you can't leverage this insight to your benefit by sharing content and suggesting your client makes contact with specific individuals within the research or advisory firms to talk about your organization. They can expect to receive an impartial and unbiased assessment of your capabilities, where you fit in relation to the competitors in the market, insights into your reputation and an objective view on the value they can expect to receive.

Step 3b: Execution of the engagement strategy

For research and intelligence gathering

I've identified five actions required to implement the engagement strategy. Initially this is aimed specifically at the intelligence-gathering phase, and then we talk about the engagement strategy for key stakeholders.

ACTION 1: PREPARATION – DEFINING OBJECTIVES, PREPARING
FOR INTERVIEWS AND CREATING THE ENGAGEMENT PLAN
Define objectives Using the information you have gathered so far from researching the organization's priorities and developing the strategy for success, you have enough to create some guiding principles around the objectives and goals of the relationship strategy. These include who you plan to talk to first, what you want to get out of the individual conversations and also what you want to learn and/or confirm about the organization.

Remember (from Chapter 1) the three core reasons why you are engaging with someone in the B2B context. They are to either 1) gather intelligence, 2) ask for an introduction (to a key decision maker or to someone who can provide some intelligence) or 3) you are directly meeting a key decision maker.

Develop an interview guide   Prepare your interview guide, which is essentially the questions you'll have in mind when you talk to these people. Although I am suggesting formal preparation for these conversations, in its simplest form this is nothing more than gathering your thoughts prior to it, and keeping in mind what it is that you are interested in learning about. As you have more of these conversations around the same topic it will flow more easily, and you will also have better context from the previous discussions. There is a wealth of information out there online about how to create interview guides and how to conduct semi-structured interviews, so explore that content to give yourself a grounding.

Create a high-level engagement plan   This is an initial plan of who you will reach out to and in which order. It doesn't need to be an exact science, with the aim of the first set of conversations usually being to complete the intelligence-gathering process. If you have some friendly people within the target organization then that is a good place to start for some informal chats. Otherwise, start with those who used to work at the target organization, then the partners and finally those currently working at the target organization. The process should begin with gathering intelligence, and then finally move on to the key stakeholders once you have a good knowledge base and can have an intelligent conversation.

ACTION 2: DECIDE WHO IS REACHING OUT AND BY WHAT COMMUNICATION CHANNEL

Now you know who you are going to engage with you need to determine the best communication channel to use.

> Remember that this is being coordinated centrally, so this includes all the people in your team. If you are anchoring these efforts you can shape the way these actions unfold.

This will be driven by the nature of the relationship and linked to how you are usually in touch with this person; based on their preferences you can determine the most effective communication channels to engage. Options may include asking for a catch-up in the form of an in-person meeting (including meeting for a coffee, a drink or dinner), email, phone calls, text/WhatsApp, video calls or social media platforms. The most likely pathway would be some form of digital communication (e.g. a LinkedIn direct message, email or text/WhatsApp) between you and the person you want to meet or, ideally, if you know them well enough, a call to them directly.

ACTION 3: CREATE CONTENT TO ATTRACT THE PERSON

This is the step where things tend to go awry as not enough thought goes into the message to intrigue the person into engaging. At this stage the objective is to open up a channel of communication, so you don't want to overcomplicate the ask or put too much information into the message. The message should be short, perhaps explaining that you are working on a project related to a particular organization and would appreciate a quick chat. Ideally, you can inject a hint of 'what's in it for you' by mentioning something related to their role, or some other information that you can share that might interest or intrigue them. The details of these things are better explained on the phone or in person, as opposed to writing a very detailed email or message. Remember, the objective of this message is to prompt them into another interaction.

ACTION 4: ENGAGE

If they respond in a positive way this is good news. You need to come to this session prepared, having reviewed the existing relationship maps, the desktop research and any other intelligence you have gathered so far about the person and the organization. This is your opportunity to present yourself as someone credible and begin to build trust. You will have your interview guide to hand; however, this should feel like a conversation rather than an 'interview'. You will have a loose structure to the way you expect the conversation to go, but the person should not feel uneasy so avoid an intense questioning style.

Hopefully it will be a cordial and friendly atmosphere when you open up the conversation, perhaps with some small talk linked to how the two people know each other. But when you get into the detail you are seeking, such as if this is a meeting to gather intelligence, remember to ask open-ended questions. People will not just volunteer insight, but an open-ended questioning style will be more likely to make them more forthcoming. For example, a line of conversation could be 'I noticed you had a new CFO start a couple of quarters ago. I listened to your most recent earnings call and they mentioned three initiatives, a), b) and c). Is one taking more of a priority at the minute?' Encourage them to share their experiences and observations based on their interactions or previous projects. In addition, encourage them to provide candid feedback and, if necessary, let them know it will remain confidential.

ACTION 5: CAPTURE INSIGHTS, REPEAT THE PROCESS AND ANALYSE THE CONTENT AS YOU GO

Although it is more and more common to record virtual meetings, I feel that people are generally still a little uncomfortable with this – especially if this is an informal conversation and you want them to share sensitive information. So, assuming it is not recorded it's important to balance capturing the key information (perhaps with a note pad) with actively listening and engaging in the conversation.

Once this first conversation is complete, work with the engagement plan for who to talk to and in which order. As mentioned, I recommend initially starting with intelligence gathering and to avoid engaging directly with the key stakeholders until you have that base knowledge, but you will be engaging with those who know the key stakeholders. This series of actions is about getting intelligence before you engage with the key stakeholders directly, and if you handle yourself well as part of the intelligence-gathering phase you tee this up for you to be able to come back on another occasion to ask for an introduction to the key stakeholder.

So, you will have notes from each of these meetings, and it's important to capture as much information as possible regarding who you talk to and what they say. The methods to do this will vary from one person to the next and one organization to the next. How you choose to do this will be based on your personal preferences to capture and store this type of information as well as your organization's internal policies. One way I'm suggesting in this book is a shared Google Sheets or Microsoft Excel spreadsheet, with key details inputted and links included to other information such as recordings of meetings.

As you complete a good number of interviews/conversations you can start to analyse the gathered information and extract key findings. Look for patterns, common themes and areas of consensus or divergence. Document these insights and observations in a way that facilitates further analysis and synthesis. These insights can be validated and cross-referenced with other sources of information, such as market research reports, industry trends or competitor insights gleaned from the desktop research.

Asking for an introduction   The sequence above is designed for those first waves of conversations when you are gathering intelligence directly from the person you are interacting with. However, there will be scenarios when you need someone to make an introduction, either to someone who can provide you some intelligence or for an introduction to a key stakeholder. This will follow a similar process as above but with some steps having a slightly different twist.

Who to ask for the introduction   There may be multiple people who know the person you want to get introduced to, and you will know some of those people better than others. But some of them know the person you want to get introduced to better than the others, so you might need to talk to a few of them before you determine the best person to help.

> Remember that because of the nature of how LinkedIn works there will be false positives. That is, there will be a lot of people who don't actually have a relationship. So, it's the panning for gold analogy I mentioned earlier. This can take a lot of effort, especially if you are trying to keep track of who you are contacting, so use your own common sense to determine how much time to invest.

Determining the best channel   If it's someone internally within your organization – and if you know them – it might be a case of seeing them in the office or catching them as part of another interaction. Otherwise, internal chat systems are the most common way to interact internally nowadays. If they are part of your external network, then it depends how well you know them and if you already have a favoured channel of communication, use that one. If there is no open line of communication, a LinkedIn direct message will have to suffice. Where possible it's always good to talk, but a digital interaction is likely to be used first to determine if they can help. However, once this has happened always try to have a quick chat on the phone or via a virtual meeting.

Content for communication   This should be brief. You want to determine if a relationship exists and, from my experience, I'd avoid asking for an introduction in the first message you send to the person you are hoping can make the introduction. If they don't know that person very well people tend to be reluctant to reach out, so avoid directly asking for an introduction in this first message. It's more of a case of asking how they know them, and their answer will give you that context. As I mentioned, if it's a LinkedIn connection be prepared for them to say they have no clue who this person is. However, if they mention that they used to work together, or they are an old college buddy or a friend, if this interaction so far has been digital then I'd suggest you now have a live conversation.

Converse with the introducer   This is a crucial action and one I often see fail. You have now determined that the introducer can help, so you need to get their support. There are usually three ways these tend to go. **First,** they can provide insight into the person such as their personality style. **Second,** once briefed they can reach out, discuss you and your organization and get feedback (without you being involved) and **third,** they can introduce you to them.

This introducer has the potential to become an ally for you as they can do one, two or all three of these things for you. Therefore, it's important that you transmit the right amount of enthusiasm and highlight the significance that the key deal, key project or key account has for you personally as well as for your organization. You need them to be willing to go out of their way to help you, and, as you can gather, this is not only time consuming but they are also putting their relationship on the line for you. Some of their willingness to help will also be about their personality, so it's not 100 per cent dependent on your relationship strength; some people are just more hardwired to help in these situations.

Engaging with key stakeholders

I want to make a clear delineation between two things. First, executing on the initial intelligence gathering phase which can be a large one-time effort to sift through all the potential leads and reach out to a lot of people to see if they can help you. Second, executing on the strategy to engage with the key stakeholders on the deal, project or account. This section assumes you have already completed that initial wave of intelligence gathering and are now ready to reach out to the stakeholders.

There is a heightened sense of importance when it comes to these conversations. At every juncture it's more important to elevate the effort and quality of what you do, so now is the time to bring to bear all of the research and intelligence you have gathered and present yourself and your organization in the strongest possible light. I've copied below a quote from Chapter 2 that typified the impact of effective research and intelligence gathering:

> What impressed me about him was the diligence with which he researched and talked to a lot of my direct reports, and a lot of other people in the business before he came to me with some ideas about making things better, even before I had thought that perhaps I had a problem. So, here was an individual who I was already beginning to trust and I just felt was somebody who I would listen to.

It's important to encapsulate as many of the qualities outlined in Chapter 2 as possible since interactions with the key stakeholders are the pinnacle of all the efforts so far. This is when you can build trust with them by demonstrating transparency, responsiveness and reliability, and by delivering on your commitments. Then you will have the chance to build your credibility and trust will quickly follow.

FIRST TALK TO THE FRIENDLIES

Now I'll point to some of the key actions to implement the engagement strategy discussed earlier in this chapter. Of all the stakeholders involved in the deal, project or account, who do you contact first? I'd suggest that the first wave are your 'friendlies'. These are the people you (or people within your organization) already have a relationship with, perhaps based on previous interactions or personal relationships built elsewhere.

Who are the people that will be happy to talk to you? If you have a lot of people who fit into this category, divide them into smaller groups so you aren't contacting too many people at the same time. We want to space these out, so as you pick up information from one conversation you can build that into the next one. Note that you will still follow the desktop research and intelligence gathering process, as having solid talking points will further increase your existing levels of credibility and trust.

Depending on the operational methods of your organization, how you get together and share information will be done in different ways. For ease of explaining, let's assume you have a diarized weekly meeting and have an internal chat channel dedicated to this deal, project or account. During the weekly meeting you decide who is going to reach out to who during the next week. This is where the profiles of key stakeholders can be used, and these will give all those involved an easy-to-interpret document to get up to speed on the individual they are taking the lead on to contact.

At the meeting the following week, updates are shared about replies and whether any conversations have happened or are planned (key information can also be shared in the internal chat channel). If some have happened, then you debrief and make sure all the information is shared and captured. This way everyone understands how this might feed into the overall objectives and how anything might inform future meetings, noting that separate internal meetings can happen for these sessions. If there are some meetings planned, then discussions turn to preparing for these interactions. Is it an informal chat on the phone or a virtual or physical meeting? If a meeting, then who should attend and what content should be shared? So, you will be going through your usual preparation and planning cycles for these meetings at the same time as reaching out to arrange new meetings.

HOW TO BUILD RELATIONSHIPS WITH THE KEY STAKEHOLDERS YOU DON'T KNOW YET

In an ideal world you start talking to the stakeholders you or your team already know and who are willing to talk to you. As these cycles of meetings happen you are gathering more intelligence that will inform future meetings, and as you go through this process you will start to build clarity on who the actual decision makers are on the deal, project or account. The key here is to be acutely aware of those you currently do not have a relationship pathway with. Sometimes, the people you know can be unwilling to bring these key stakeholders into the conversation or make an introduction, and this can be very common at the early stages, especially if it's their boss or someone very senior. In these instances, you will need to use the relationships you have as a conduit to these people.

> There is nothing wrong with sending a LinkedIn invitation with a short note saying who you are working with and on what. Do keep in very brief though, no more than 30 words. Often, they'll accept the invite and that can sometimes lead to a dialogue. However, be wary of this being perceived as 'going behind the back' of your key contact. You don't want to jeopardize a relationship you have put a lot of effort into building.

Find those who have the clearest route to the key stakeholder and treat them as the proxy to that relationship. Keep building value and contextualizing the conversation to what they need, as they'll be passing this information up the chain and will, perhaps, be informing you of the feedback from the executive. So, you are having a relationship through their trusted lieutenant, and this scenario is completely normal. At the same time, you can be working the back channels through your partner ecosystem to see if you can influence the key stakeholder in a similar way, perhaps through someone senior on your side, a partner or an existing client that you know has a relationship with them. Such information can be identified through the intelligence-gathering phase.

CONTACTING COLD

My philosophy is, whenever possible, to leverage an existing relationship – that is the purpose of this book. However, it doesn't always work out like that! So, when there are no existing relationships the last resort is to contact them directly. In simple terms, you need to find out the key burning issues that person is trying to solve. This is where your desktop research and intelligence-gathering activities will be key, and then engage them with the value you can bring to the table to help them solve that problem.

Step 3c: Shifting from org chart to relationship map

At the end of Chapter 4 we created an initial org chart to visualize the current view of the existing relationships within the target client. Since then, through Chapters 5 and 6 we've built out a broad view of who has the potential to help, and these are the existing relationships. We now want to make the shift from an org chart to a relationship map. Initially, on the first cycle of analysis it might be a rather rudimentary view as you wouldn't know too much yet. However, that is okay as it's just the base view, and with each cycle through the relationship-mapping process more detail will flow in as the depth and breadth of knowledge increases.

The relationship map provides the opportunity to visually articulate the relationship strategy, especially to a wider audience such as the organizational C-suite. It's important to have a mechanism to highlight key insights, the key players supporting the process and the progress being made towards the identified objectives and relationship strategy. The relationship map forms part of that.

The relationship map will also showcase who from your side is engaging with who from the client side. Perhaps most significantly, this map identifies the key people from the client side and how they are helping, and these are the all-important internal champions. Real progress is made with key deals, key projects and within key accounts when you have such people on your

FIGURE 6.1 Relationship map

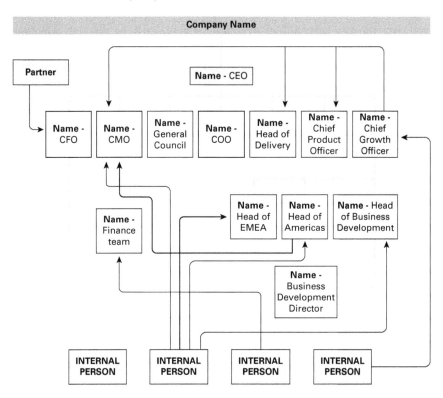

side within the client organization. So, to summarize, the relationship map overlays the following on top of the org chart:

- Who is working for you internally.
- Who on your side is part of the team and who are they paired with on the client side.
- Which partners are supporting you and who are they targeting.
- Other external people on the team (advisers, industry experts, existing clients).

Figure 6.1 provides an example of a simplified relationship map with the detail removed from the boxes to make it easier to illustrate. The point this map is articulating is to identify who from your side is aligned with who from the client side, and then identify which people the champions on the client side are engaging with on your behalf.

Be aware that using spreadsheets can become unmanageable as these relationship maps get bigger and more complicated. This is especially true when adding your own lines, so you will need to shift to an org chart software at some stage.

Capturing and presenting this insight

There are **four separate parts** to this: tracking information, snapshots, extending the details and collating a status summary.

The **first** part is a snapshot of the **relationship map** we just discussed. While the map itself is a living document, as part of your regular weekly meetings you can take a snapshot of the map and use this to explain the overall strategy and the gameplan for the short, medium and long term.

The **second** is a document that acts as a **tracker** of who from your side is contacting who from the client side. Extending the Microsoft Excel or Google Sheets spreadsheet I've referenced in this same section in Chapters 4 and 5, I create a column for each week of the internal meeting. Each row lines up to one of the key stakeholders and then you track who is reaching out to who. There are four things to collect: the owner of the outreach, the action, the date and the outcome. I tend to use colour coding here too to denote when something is positive (green) or negative (red), amber if it is in motion, and then white to denote that nothing has been started yet. Figure 6.2 provides a snapshot of what this could look like. It's important to note that this is more of an administrative document rather than something you would publish to the wider internal team. Also note that the actual template document I can share is an extension of the one presented in Figure 4.2 and should also contain details from the desktop research and intelligence gathering as part of Step 2. The content from all three steps is contained within one master tracker document.

FIGURE 6.2 Document to plan and track the stakeholder engagement

Client Individual	WEEK 1				WEEK 2			
	Owner	Action	Date	Outcome	Owner	Action	Date	Outcome
name 1	Owner	Action	Date	Outcome	Owner	Action	Date	Outcome
name 2								
name 3								
name 4								
name 5								

The **third** part involves extending the details within the **stakeholder profiles** you created as part of the research and intelligence-gathering efforts in Step 2. You will be capturing more information from the conversations, so this can be used to update these profiles. These profiles, along with the relationship map, are used as the basis of the internal conversation when deciding who will reach out to who, so the profile will give them the base context they need.

The **fourth** part is pulling the key details from this chapter and combining with major outcomes from this section in Chapters 4 and 5 to create an overview or **status summary**. Your management, key stakeholders and the wider team will want to understand how well you as an organization are aligned to the client as well as wanting details on progress on the deal, project or account. This means creating separate content, often in Microsoft PowerPoint or Google Slides, so it will involve copying over datapoints and snapshots of the maps to tell the story.

Repeating steps 1, 2 and 3

There is a sense of there being a 'cycle of continuous improvement' with regards to this relationship-mapping process. You identify the key stakeholders as part of Step 1, you conduct research and intelligence gathering as part of Step 2 (which might identify more names to populate Step 1) and you engage with them in Step 3. Importantly, Step 3 will almost certainly identify more names for Step 1, and you then begin the research and intelligence-gathering phase again. However, you will also be doing periodic research and intelligence gathering on all of the existing stakeholders to further inform those conversations as they progress.

What we've learned in this chapter

Within this chapter we have learned:

- What an engagement strategy is.
- The three elements to Step 3:
  o 3a: the importance of multi-threading.
  o 3b: execution of the engagement strategy.
  o 3c: the shift to a relationship map.

What's coming next

Next comes the final part of the book where we put everything together around the three use cases we have been discussing (key deals, key projects and key accounts) and set you on the path to putting this into action.

PART THREE

Putting the relationship-mapping process into action

The next four chapters form Part 3 of this book, with Part 1 having set the stage as to why relationships are important and Part 2 explaining the relationship-mapping process. Now, Part 3 is about bringing things to life and is broken down as follows:

- Chapter 7 considers relationship maps in the context of key deals.
- Chapter 8 considers relationship maps in the context of key projects.
- Chapter 9 considers relationship maps in the context of key accounts.
- Chapter 10 discusses implementing the process and taking it to the next level.

Chapter 7 tells you how to use relationship maps to win deals, from sourcing them, to qualifying them, to managing them through the sales process, to winning them – and how key relationships will support you each step of the way. Once you have won these deals, what happens next? Chapter 8 is about successfully delivering the project. If the project fails then the relationship is likely to be severely impacted and if that happens, then all of the effort to win the deal is wasted – so building and maintaining key stakeholder relationships is vital.

This brings us on to Chapter 9 which considers all of what we have learned so far in the context of effective key account management. Considering that most of an organization's revenue comes from a relatively small number of accounts, taking proper care of those key accounts is paramount. There is an interdependence between winning deals, delivering successful projects and building and maintaining relationships with the executives and key stakeholders within a key account. And for a successfully managed key account this will be a continuous cycle. Finally, Chapter 10 pulls together everything that has been discussed so far and explains what to do now, so then you can put this book down and start mapping your relationships.

Case studies at the end of Chapters 7, 8 and 9

At the end of Chapters 7, 8 and 9 there will be a section for case studies explaining how the relationship-mapping process was put into action. As you can probably imagine, if we went into the minute details of each key deal, key project or key account we could probably fill a whole book on each one. So, as much as possible the focus is on the relationship and explaining how that impacted the process, rather than presenting the case studies as a model of best practice on how to do things most effectively. As has been discussed multiple times so far, identifying and aligning to the corporate, unit and individual priorities is an absolute must. So, please assume this was being constantly evaluated and recalibrated throughout each case study.

The case studies are set up to showcase how, over the course of many months (and actually years), the cycle through the relationship-mapping process was repeated, and by doing so this presented more insight into the stakeholders. This led to more research and intelligence gathering and then to better engagement, and the cycle continued until the outcome was reached. So, for the cycles I did my best to break the timeline down into what seemed like the natural cycle of the process.

A key insight from the write-up of these case studies is the actual amount of time and effort that goes into them, from first conversation to an end outcome. It can often be years – and in some cases many years – and inside that timeline are thousands of interactions, be they emails, calls or meetings. Going through this data and putting it together was a painstaking but very awakening experience, especially when there seems to be such a focus in today's market on 'moving the pipeline' or 'cleaning out the pipeline'. The reality is that these outcomes often outlast some of the key stakeholders on both the client and the supplier side, which makes the subject of this book even more valid.

As you will see, the outcomes are not all positive. Personally, I learn a lot more when things do not go to plan versus the successes. The case studies are based on real examples from my experiences but have been adapted and generalized. Please note that there is no link between the chapter introductions for Chapters 7, 8 and 9 and the case study for that chapter.

7

Relationship maps applied to key deals

Introduction

ADRIAN BARNWELL, DELOITTE – STRATEGIC SALES COACH

Big deals can affect the share price of both the buyer and seller and have more in common with mergers and acquisitions than they do with typical run rate orders. There's more money involved, more people and greater complexity, and creating and sustaining momentum from inception to close is like rolling a big rock up a steep hill. Successful deal makers (or rainmakers) are, therefore, rare beasts. What special attributes do they have? What do they focus on to win? In my experience, while there are many things to think about, successful rainmakers do three things really, really well.

First, many think they spend their time walking the corridors of power, wining and dining executives, and there's certainly some of that. But while executives enjoy a nice burgundy, they can get those elsewhere. Successful rainmakers recognize that meaningful relationships are initially formed around thought leadership or sense-making, which often involves bringing a fresh or counter perspective to the table. Too often, so-called thought leadership is just a 'me too' perspective. Saying that AI will be used a lot in the future isn't particularly helpful, but a lot of organizations make these statements of the obvious. It's one reason executives are confused by the plethora of noisy opinions out there.

What is important is addressing the question of what does all that mean for me? Rainmakers recognize the value of original thinking applied to their prospect's organization, or for the individual they're sitting opposite. It's *very specific* and is designed to create or provoke a discussion. Really good thought leadership makes executives sit back in their chair, taken aback by your prediction of the future. It doesn't matter if they disagree, what matters is that they're entering a debate with you to understand more. Imagine if Kodak's executives had reacted to the world of digital, Nokia had done something with the knowledge that software had become more important than form factor or Blockbuster had understood the value of streaming years before their respective demises. Thought leadership isn't about selling your organization's products or services. It's about demonstrating through your ability to hold the debate that you're someone who can help your prospect progress, both at an individual and organizational level. As such, it's the catalyst for a collaboration.

This brings us to the second area rainmakers focus on, that of relationships. All organizations run on politics and personal agendas, and decisions aren't made in meetings but rather in corridors. They're made by emotions not logic (which catches up afterwards to justify things). Big deals face huge scrutiny, with lots of stakeholders influencing the ultimate decision makers. Knowing how to navigate this environment and create decision momentum is what separates successful rainmakers from the rest. Rainmakers don't rely on subjective opinions about relationships, they measure the valuable actions prospects take on their behalf to move things forward. Are they guiding and coaching you? Do they provide competitive intelligence? Are they collaborating with you on their business case or to improve your value proposition? No big deal succeeds without at least one, highly influential, senior executive as your ally. They sell for you when you're not in the room: opening doors, making things happen and neutralizing your competitors' allies (your detractors).

While our first two rainmaker areas of focus are logical, the third is a softer attribute of their personal make up. Rainmakers have high emotional intelligence. They know themselves well and have admirable self-control and self-confidence, regardless of their audience. They approach each internal or client meeting as if they have a pipeline full of highly qualified, excellent deals and are already ahead of target (they probably are). They also have zero emotional attachment to a deal and rely on inputs to objectively form a view. Such an approach means they're ruthless in time management and, therefore, deal qualification and if a deal isn't progressing they'll quickly cut their investment in it. Rainmakers know that while it's helpful to be liked – it's certainly better than not being liked – their prospects need to like what they can do for them. They also don't get hung up by organizational hierarchy and when they meet a CEO, they view it as a meeting of equals – two experts in their fields, exchanging ideas.

Finding good big deals is like searching for a needle in a haystack. When rainmakers meet that CEO, they're not selling, they're sorting. Does this prospect meet my criteria for us to work together? They don't accept a load of actions to please the CEO and know that if the CEO is serious, they'll take their share of the actions. Deal making is a leadership role, for your organization and your prospect's. Leadership is sometimes described as the art of creating followership in others and if you build the right relationships they will follow.

What is a key deal?

From the **client's** perspective a key deal is an initiative that is expected to have a **transformational impact** on their business. It should provide better **market positioning** by allowing them to better serve their customers, expand their market share or enter new markets, all of which is really about providing them with a **competitive advantage**. Usually, a key deal has the promise of **growing revenue** or **reducing their costs**, and sometimes it has both. So, the client believes it will create significant long-term value for them and will help them align with their **core business objectives** and strategic goals.

From the **supplier's** perspective a key deal is one that is **strategically important**. This can mean it aligns to the strategic objectives and growth plans such as entering **new markets**, expanding into a **new sector** or creating a **new offering**; essentially, anything that would enhance the supplier's competitive position and grow their market share. On the other hand, it could be a deal with a **key client,** a key prospect or a key partner. If the deal involves collaborating with a major player that holds significant influence, reputation or market presence, then it makes sense to consider it a key deal. This is because association with this organization will add credibility, bring visibility in the market and provide high potential for future business opportunities.

Key strategic deals are expected to have a **long-term impact** on the supplier's business and tend to involve a commitment that extends beyond the short term. This demonstrates that they are invested in making it a success, so to that end these are usually multi-year agreements with options to extend again built into the contract. Such deals require the organization to deliver a **complex solution** that addresses specific needs and challenges. This may involve integrating various products, services and technologies, or expertise from different business units within the organization.

These deals can attract **significant competition** from others, often fierce competitors, so the process can become highly competitive and can have an impact on your market positioning if you win and if you lose. Finally, these types of strategic deals often have substantial **financial implications**. They typically have a high contract value, in proportion to your organization's typical deal size, and they also tend to involve significant financial investments from the supplier too. Winning or losing such a deal will impact financial performance: if you are a small start-up a key deal could be worth $50,000 and if you are a global corporation, then a key deal could be hundreds of millions or even billions of dollars over a longer-term agreement. These numbers are sometimes hard to fathom, but take a look at the annual revenue of some of the largest organizations in the world and you will see they are well into the hundreds of billions per year, so then a billion-dollar multi-year deal seems less outlandish.

How to win key deals

Throughout Part 2 of this book, we've discussed the importance of understanding the client's **objectives**, developing a **win strategy** and defining and **engaging with the key stakeholders** involved in the deal, project or account. The importance of understanding and aligning to client priorities and objectives cannot be overstated, but we cover that more in the next two use cases. There are some specific elements that you need to get right to have any chance of winning the key deal. Most of these were highlighted within Chapter 2, and it's important to remember that they are not sequential and various elements can be worked on at the same time. It's also important to consider these in the context that the biggest reason a client does not select your organization is not because they chose a competitor, but rather because they decided to do nothing at all and keep the status quo.

Credentials to deliver

Having solid experience and a good track record of delivering similar types of solutions is paramount when it comes to winning key deals, with clients placing a significant emphasis on this. They want assurance that the chosen organization has the necessary knowledge and expertise and will want evidence of similar implementations delivered successfully. This is because a proven track record instils confidence. If you are an incumbent supplier, the track record of success would hopefully be easier to point to, but if you are a new supplier these credentials will need to be evidenced through other means.

Mapping relationships identifies the stakeholders that have the biggest concerns about this, and whom others internally on the client side are looking to for validation that the supplier indeed does have the necessary experience. Once these people are identified, engaging with them directly to present case studies, set up reference calls or to share other insights will provide the assurances and satisfy their concerns.

Solution fit

How well the solution that you present aligns with the client's needs and objectives and how it solves their pain points is central to your success. Clients will consider the comprehensiveness of your solution and will want to stress test it to ensure it covers all necessary aspects and requirements. A strong solution fit showcases the supplier's ability to provide a tailored solution.

Mapping relationships allows you to identify the stakeholders who have a deep understanding of their organization's needs and pain points, and by engaging in meaningful conversations with these stakeholders you can gather valuable insights and align your solution more effectively. Developing these relationships allows you to get to the details that will enable you to create a powerful winning solution.

Risk mitigation

This could be considered an extension of the solution, but because of its significance it is worth raising as a separate point. Depending on the risk appetite and maturity of the client organization they'll have existing systems and processes in place that need to be adhered to. These can include data privacy and information security protocols, regulatory and compliance requirements, robust contingency procedures and other such assessments of risk. Any perceived risks need to be understood and approved for a deal to move forward.

Mapping relationships helps identify stakeholders who are responsible for risk management within the client's organization. Often, these people are process driven so engaging in open dialogues about any identified risks, the options for mitigation and their compliance measures allows you to understand their process. From this you can create a coherent plan to mini-mize or mitigate these risks to a level they are comfortable with.

A strong value proposition

This is a critical factor in the decision-making process. Clients need to understand the value that will be realized by the proposed solution. They'll be creating a business case to support the funding for this solution and will assess the ROI potential, cost-effectiveness and the competitive edge the supplier solution will provide them.

Mapping relationships enables you to identify stakeholders who are influential in determining the value proposition. It's important that you are working side by side with them almost as part of the same team. This is because an understanding of the value drivers and return on investment metrics that are important to the client will enable you to effectively articu-late where and how your solution will fit. Critically, it will also address the financial impact it will deliver. These elements must be strongly evidenced in the proposal.

Quality of resources

The client being convinced you have done this before and have presented a solid solution is one thing, but them being convinced you can do it for them is another. This is dependent on the capabilities of the team assigned to the project along with the availability of necessary resources. They are often referenced as the A team versus the B team with the distinction made based on the client's assessment of the expertise and experience of the core team. The client will evaluate their ability to successfully execute the project based on their experience and judgement. From that they can determine if is this an A team or a B team, or in some cases maybe a C or a D team. The suppli-er's wider ability to support the project will also be under scrutiny, including the support functions, while assessment of whether or not the supplier is overstretching is also a possibility.

Mapping relationships identifies the stakeholders responsible for this, so you can address head-on by presenting the team and providing the opportu-nity for them to get to know each other, or better still including people on the team they already know and trust. It helps if you are in the position to confirm that these are the people who will be on the delivery team, as this will instil confidence in the client.

References and client testimonials

Clients often seek to corroborate what the supplier is telling them by validating it with previous clients. This can be in various forms, such as shared written or video testimonials or a formal reference call. These offer a valuable and unique perspective on the supplier's ability to do as they are promising, with clients tending to place considerable weight on this insight.

Mapping relationships helps you to identify the right people from the references side. You will probably need to talk to people internally if they hold the relationship and convince them to help you. If the person giving the reference is senior and at a large organization, they'll be busy, and there may also be multiple requests coming to this person. So, you may need to negotiate well to get your internal colleagues to support you with this request as quite often they will be reluctant to ask their client for too many reference calls.

Cultural fit

As this is a strategic project, how the two companies will fit together is very important. Depending on the size and scale of the deal it can be almost like a marriage, so clients seek a strong working relationship based on trust, effective communication and shared values. They'll be evaluating your organization vis-à-vis their own values as cultural fit is also a driver for successful collaboration, and that is central to the overall success of the partnership.

Mapping relationships helps identify the stakeholders that can provide insights into the organization's culture and values. The more people you meet the better your understanding becomes of the cultural nuances, not only from asking but also from what you observe when you meet people.

Innovation and investments in the future

Now more than ever clients recognize that if you are standing still, you are moving backwards. As such, partnering with someone who is investing in the future demonstrates commitment to innovation and future readiness. While it's very difficult to know precisely where the industry or market is heading, having an open mind and showcasing your willingness to adapt to and embrace change is an important factor.

Mapping relationships helps identify the stakeholders that are responsible for innovation and future readiness within the client organization. These conversations should also extend to the C-suite who will have their own views. Aligning your subject matter experts to these stakeholders will help you to understand and align to their vision for the future while also advising the client based on your point of view.

Financial stability

This has some overlap with the point on risk, but it's also worthwhile addressing it separately. It's a crucial consideration as clients want assurance that the supplier is financially stable and capable of fulfilling all contractual obligations. As part of this they'll want to review the supplier's financial statements, credit ratings, market position and overall financial health. It is also worth noting that a client should not want to push a supplier to the financial limit; that is not in their interests at all.

Mapping relationships helps by following the same pattern of identifying the right stakeholders who have insights into what is important and form part of the decision-making criteria, ideally before formally sharing details. If there are any weak points these can be navigated by working with and getting the support from key stakeholders before any final decisions are made.

Commercials and contract terms

You will often hear clients say that while pricing is an important consideration it's not the sole determining factor, and it's true that the price is always in the context of the overall value proposition. The term 'commercials' extends to other elements beyond the price itself, namely the pricing structure and payment terms as well as contractual conditions such as liability exposure, termination clauses and indemnities. Each of these items has the potential to derail a deal, so it's a very delicate and often tedious process.

Mapping relationships identifies the right stakeholders to deal with but, crucially, it's the quality of the relationships that matters. It's important form that you understand their budgetary constraints and hard objections within the contract terms versus negotiation positions. Often, this can be a difficult tightrope to balance on but if the right level of trust has been built and there is enough of a willingness to make the deal happen, then it's at this stage that all the key relationships which have been developed need to be considered and effectively leveraged.

How to source key deals

In this section I'll highlight some of the steps to follow to source key deals and, more importantly, how your existing relationship network can support this process. But before we go deeper into how to source key deals, it's important to recognize that the deals themselves originate from different places. Where they come from, and indeed who is driving that, to a large degree determines how you can source these types of deals, and I'd argue that it also determines how successful you will be in winning. I'd like to build this out across three phases:

- First, there is having the idea to actually do something – how does the client know they need your solution?
- Second, there is the selection process and making the decision as to who will deliver the solution.
- Third, there is the renewal of the contract to deliver or maintain the solution.

Defining who you should engage with

The journey to making a decision to do something can be a complex one for a client and, as previously highlighted, the number one reason why a client doesn't move forward is because they decide to do nothing. However, let's start this from the position that your organization has an idea that they think will provide significant value should a client adopt it, so you are taking this idea to the market without the client coming to you. This can be anything from a process change to a services solution or a software product (or a combination of all three); the 'what it is' part doesn't matter as much as the 'how to source it' part.

One of the first things you need to determine is who this solution is relevant for. If you have got this far in the book it might not be a surprise to learn that that the answer is research. In this case, market research. Conducting thorough market research to identify industries and sectors that align with your organization's solution helps to focus the energy of your organization in the right place. This would extend to the decision makers your solution impacts and why, as well as the business case to support the decision.

Desktop research is the obvious place to start and that should extend to talking to your existing relationship network to further validate what you have found. You would then need to create some content that positions your organization as a thought leader, something which is done to establish it as an expert in this space. Whether that is creating content such as white papers, research articles, case studies or blog posts, it should promote your expertise. Cultivating any existing relationships with industry influencers and experts will help you to amplify this message to the market. They can share your content, endorse your expertise or invite you to contribute to industry publications or speaking engagements, all of which will increase your visibility and attract potential clients.

Creating new pipelines

It shouldn't be any surprise that the first place I suggest you go is to your existing clients, who are often willing to test new solutions. Within your client base you already have existing relationships, hopefully with a good track record and good levels of trust, so there should be some receptiveness to your proposition. The approach we discussed within Part 2 should be applied here as well as when you take the idea to prospective clients. So, it would be a case of identifying and mapping the key stakeholders, conducting research and intelligence gathering, and then implementing the engagement strategy to develop the relationships.

Another route to source key deals is leveraging strategic partnerships and alliance relationships. Spend time identifying those you can form an alliance with; these should complement your offerings and have existing relationships with your target markets. In addition, consider services that might be able to build your offering into one of their solutions. Collaborate with these partners to pursue joint opportunities and leverage each other's networks and expertise. You can use your existing relationships to help you engage with the identified strategic partners, and then use the relationship-mapping process to properly identify, map and develop the relationships.

Hosting and attending events, either in-person or online, is another common way of building pipeline, and there is an obvious preference for in-person events. If I'm being honest, when it comes to creating new pipeline, I haven't seen a huge volume of quality leads coming from sponsoring and attending events. Sometimes it is just about 'being there'. In marketing terms, the justification for the cost of events can often be the negative impact of not being there – attendees don't see your brand and might assume that you are not a player in the space. I do, however, find them to be fantastic ways to develop existing relationships, and as part of those conversations you can ask them to introduce you to other key stakeholders that happen to be in attendance too. From that perspective they can be very helpful. In that same spirit, I've had success over the years with developing existing relationships through roundtable sessions with either breakfast or lunch/dinner options. These can be arranged jointly with someone from your partner ecosystem or done on your own, but they need to be focused on thought leadership and peer-to-peer networking for the attendees. These are a good opportunity for a touchpoint with a key stakeholder.

Co-creation with the client

The last section explored the scenario where you have an idea and want to take it to the market. However, this can be a long-drawn-out process: you need to find the right people, explain the problem or the pain points and then introduce your value proposition. There are also various stages to the maturity curve: some might not know they have a problem; some people will know they have pain but not know how to solve it; and some will know they have an issue and be thinking about how to solve it. In addition, others will have done all of that and already be using a competitor.

For those who know they have a problem and are thinking about how to solve it, there is an opportunity to work closely with the client to co-create a solution. This can take various forms and involve various degrees of time, effort and investment from the involved parties. If you meet the right person at the right time a conversation like this could also stem from the 'creating new pipelines' activities above.

However, it tends to happen when a client and supplier already have an existing relationship, with this close bond creating trust from which innovation and dynamism can flow. When this happens it's a fantastic opportunity to position your organization as a tailored solution, to integrate yourself into their processes and align solidly to their objectives and outcomes.

The supplier selection process

If you have done a good enough job of working with the right stakeholders to create a bespoke solution that is integrated into the client's way of working and all the right people are supportive and aligned, then the obvious next step is to agree the contract and start the project. But if only it were that simple. Anyone involved in the deal-making process for any amount of time, especially strategic deals with a significant amount of value attached, knows that before the deal is made someone within the client organization is going to ask, 'so who else can do this?'.

Now if you have been working with this particular client on this solution for months (sometimes years) and investing significant amounts of time and money, this can be a very uncomfortable conversation for the client to have with you. Of course, if there is an opportunity to avoid this then do pursue that (it's not unheard of for clients to use this as a negotiation angle too). However, due to various reasons such as the size of the deal and compliance reasons or just peace of mind that they are making the right decision, sometimes the client will talk to other suppliers. This may seem like a step backwards but if it has to happen it can actually be a good thing.

The 'who else can do this?' conversation might not always result in a formal process where the client requests proposals from other suppliers. Sometimes it can be done more informally and if you were selected as the winner after this 'informal' process of talking to other suppliers and industry experts, then I'm sure you would be very pleased. However, if you weren't then that would be another story and you would have preferred something more structured and transparent. Which leads us to the requests-for-proposals (RFP) process.

The RFP process

Depending on the size and scale of the project the process can start with a request for information (RFI), also known as a pre-qualification questionnaire. An RFI is typically used in the early stages of a procurement process and, as the name suggests, is when a buyer is gathering information about potential suppliers and their capabilities. RFIs usually ask for general information about a supplier's products, services, capabilities, experience and other relevant details. This may also include questions about the supplier's financial stability, references and qualifications in relation to the scope they are considering. They don't usually include pricing information since the primary goal is to gather information and create a shortlist of potential suppliers for the RFP.

The RFP process is more formal and detailed and is used when a buyer is ready to ask for proposals from potential suppliers for a specific and defined scope of work, project or contract. It includes a detailed description of the buyer's needs as well as the specifications and requirements of the project. They often include specific criteria for evaluating proposals such as technical specifications, delivery timelines, pricing and contractual terms. However, the decision criteria are not always shared with suppliers, with one example being how easy the client foresees it will be to do business with a given supplier. Nonetheless, for government and other publicly funded contracts the decision process, criteria and feedback process are much more transparent. The format comprises two aspects. One is a formal submission process of physical documents (Microsoft Word, PowerPoint and Excel) which can sometimes be submitted via email or could be through a specially designed portal. The other is via question and answer (Q&A) type discussions and can be face-to-face or virtual, and can also be one-to-one or through a group discussion. These are not sequential, and you could have a Q&A then the submission, then more Q&A and other conversations to evaluate your response.

Why clients run an RFP process

There are several reasons why a client would run an RFP. By inviting proposals from multiple suppliers based on the same scope and same information they are able to standardize the process, and thereby evaluate the different options against the best pricing, the best solution and overall best fit for their organization. Because there is competition, organizations tend to be more aggressive with their commercials, and by comparing the different pricing models they can negotiate the most favourable terms and select the supplier that offers the best value for their budget. As such, the client should secure the best value for money. The decision-making process includes an evaluation of factors, such as financial stability, references and past performance. Sometimes there are also internal rules about awarding contracts above a certain value.

By evaluating proposals from different suppliers, organizations can gain insights into industry standards and best practices as well as emerging trends. This helps them assess their own processes, capabilities and performance, potentially leading to improvements in their own operations. It can also help achieve a much better understanding of the industry from an outside-in perspective, and this allows them to incorporate any new innovations into their solution. Consequently, they can futureproof themselves and bring added value to the solution, thus creating a better competitive advantage for their business.

Lastly but certainly not least, it's to get internal stakeholders involved in, aligned with and part of the decision-making process. With stakeholders from different departments and functions, the organization can ensure that the selected supplier aligns with the needs and priorities of the various stakeholder groups. This promotes buy-in and consensus among the different teams and increases the likelihood of a successful outcome.

The value of being there first

To pick up from earlier in the chapter, if you are taking the idea to the client in the first place or are involved to some degree in co-creating the idea with the client and it does end up going to an RFP process, then you are obviously in a much stronger position compared to anyone else invited into the process at a later date. Not least it demonstrates that you are a leader and an innovator in that specific sphere, and you have more time to prepare and tailor your solution. As is the central concept of this book, crucially, you have established relationships with the buying organization – perhaps not with everyone but with enough of the key stakeholders for them to take it seriously and take it forward.

In addition, the levels of credibility and trust you have built will help at each stage of the process, not only with the key stakeholder but with others across the organization. When you introduce the idea or are involved in its creation, you have a much better understanding of the problem, its impact and the potential solutions. And when these are being formulated into the scope for the RFP you could have influence on the structure, the specifications and the evaluation criteria, ideally making it easier to showcase your strengths and your unique value proposition. This is obviously a delicate balance between understanding that the client must run a fair and impartial process, and the inputs and insight you happen to have by virtue of the fact you have been there from the beginning. How much influence you have in shaping the details of the RFP document is another thing, but worst case you will have a more detailed view on the drivers for this initiative and who the key stakeholders are that are making the decision.

Reasons for the client to avoid an RFP

If you have built enough trust with the client and are aligned on the objectives and scope then it could be useful, as a last effort, to explain to them that going through an RFP process is also a drain on their side (as well as yours). The whole end-to-end RFP process takes a considerable amount of time, and if there is an urgent need this delay could impact their timeline to value. As well as resources from both sides it's also hugely resource intensive for the client. They are required to draft a detailed RFP, manage supplier queries and thoroughly assess the received proposals.

The resources needed for this are not only time but also financial, and these resources could potentially be utilized more effectively in core business operations and delivering the project under discussion. There is an argument to be made that an RFP process can be too structured and formal as well as being too quantitative, with not enough focus on the intangibles such as relationship quality and trust, and your willingness to adapt and be flexible as the project needs dictate. If what the client is planning has a significant competitive advantage then running an RFP will announce this to the market, so that first mover advantage is lost. All too often these processes end up with decision paralysis, with too many people involved who have too many personal agendas and with too many variables.

When an RFP comes to you

When this happens, you need to make some strategic decisions, and there are many scenarios where this could happen. One is the scenario outlined above: in its worst interpretation the client would like to do a deal with a particular supplier but because of compliance reasons or other factors they need to go through an RFP process before formally agreeing to work with their preferred supplier. Another scenario could be that the client has made a decision to pursue this project without influence from a supplier, and now they need to evaluate the market to identify a partner to work with, or perhaps this is a renewal of an existing contract. Based on the size and scale of the project, for the reasons mentioned above these are sometimes required (or there is a preference) to go through an RFP process to ensure the client is getting the best value.

In any of these scenarios you may be approached by the organization itself, hear about it another way such as a public procurement portal or from a deal adviser or other third party. It's common with much larger strategic deals for the client to work with an external party to help them navigate through this very complex process. Part of the role of the deal adviser is to identify the key players in the market that could fulfil the requirements of the proposal, and they'll reach out and invite you to respond. So, your relationship with deal advisers is very important, and depending on the strength of the relationship they may be willing to be more open with you about the reality of the competitive landscape.

As outlined above, when you respond to a formal RFP it's a huge investment of time and resources and shouldn't be taken lightly. For large contracts the cost to just respond can often be millions of dollars without any guarantee you will be awarded any business. This figure is made up of the cost of the team assigned to respond, with the end-to-end process taking one to two years (or even longer), plus the travel budget for meetings onsite with the client as well as other costs to support the process. So, it's a big investment and you need to be sure you can make that financial investment but also, and perhaps more importantly, is the opportunity cost of focusing resources on this and not some other opportunity. In particular, if you are a smaller organization, you might not be spending millions of dollars, but you need to make sure your limited resources are not wasted.

Therefore, it becomes an assessment exercise as to how this aligns with your business strategy and objectives. In completing this exercise make sure you understand the scope, requirements, timelines to deliver and the evaluation criteria. You need to be sure that your organization has the capabilities and resources to not only respond but to deliver, based on which you will be able to make an assessment of your potential for success. This will be influenced by the competitor landscape; sometimes clients are open (either formally or informally) about who else is bidding in the RFP process, and you can use this information to make an assessment.

Bid or no-bid on RFPs

This has been a quite protracted explanation of how the opportunity to win key deals can originate, but it was to get to the point that all roads lead back to relationships. All other things being equal, the opportunities you pursue are driven by the quality of the existing relationships with the organization as a whole and, more importantly, the key stakeholders on the deal. This isn't to say you need to have strong relationships with all the key stakeholders from day one, not at all. Perhaps you have very few relationships but if you know a key deal is coming in the future or that a large renewal with a key competitor is coming up, you can start to plan for this well in advance. Indeed, if you have 6, 12 or even 18 months' lead time before the RFP is even released, you can take the initiative to build those key relationships ahead of time.

By following the relationship-mapping process outlined in Part 2 you will be able to identify, map and try to develop those key stakeholder relationships.

If they respond positively to your overtures you can make a judgement based on that, and you can also make a judgement based on the fact they aren't interested in building a relationship with you and your organization. So, the quality of these relationships drives your decision to bid on the RFP or not. This principle holds true for anytime you hear about the RFP process. As discussed throughout this book, for you to be successful you need to have a good flow of intelligence and with an RFP, more than anything else, you need to have intelligence on the competitive landscape. Thus, the quality of the information you receive is directly related to the quality of your relationships.

Summary of examples for leveraging existing relationships for key deals

Qualifying in or out of a deal

As just discussed, considering the investment of time, effort and money that goes into trying to win a deal, you had better be sure to be spending your organization's limited resources wisely. We know that the decision about who to select (or indeed whether to stay in the status quo) will be made by a set of named individuals. So, right at the time you are deciding whether you should bid for this work or not it's important to incorporate into that decision the strength of the relationships with the key stakeholders making the decision. Now, if you don't know who the key stakeholders are then that is a problem, so you need to find that out before making the decision.

If it's a scenario where you have relationships with some or all of the key stakeholders and their direct reports (plus others within the organization), it becomes a question of the quality of those relationships (and the quality of the information they share with you) versus the footprint and position of any competitors. If you have that full picture and believe you have a good probability to win the deal, then it makes sense to pursue it. If it's not the case, then it depends on the risk appetite you are prepared to accept.

Identify 'unknown' existing relationships to support the deal

No matter the quality of the relationships you already have, as anyone that has been involved in trying to win deals for any amount of time can attest, it can be just one relationship that makes the difference in winning the deal. This is especially true in highly competitive situations. So, going through the process outlined in Part 2 permits the opportunity to do a relationship audit and identify stakeholders outside of your circle as well as that of the core team. These are individuals who can bring intelligence, and if they are senior executives they could bring influence too.

Monitor key stakeholder engagement throughout the deal cycle

With the deal in-flight and the win strategy being executed on, Step 3 of the relationship-mapping process is the relationship engagement strategy. Making sure this engagement is happening in the right sequence is crucial to the success of the deal, and you are almost like the conductor of an orchestra in this regard. Creating an overall picture of who you are engaging with and when will help to synchronize the activities and be more coordinated in the overall approach.

Case study 1: Country-level agreement with a global consulting organization

Client: a global accounting and consulting organization present in over 100 countries. While this organization operates as one global brand it's actually made up of multiple separate legal entities, usually formed at a country level. This key deal was with one of the major countries within the overall global network, and the supplier already had agreements with two other countries in the network.

Supplier: organization selling enterprise software.

Deal value: this was the largest deal of the year and was in the top 10 of all deals won in the organization's history (the supplier having been established for more than 10 years).

Timeline: from first conversation at the start of this deal cycle to the signed agreement was two years and six months.

Relationship capital invested: this section is to highlight the amount of time that was put into this process by the key contact, who in this case was also the champion on the client side (but the key person isn't always the champion). Over the total timeframe of this deal – which was two years and six months – the key contact exchanged almost **600 emails** and attended more than **40 meetings** with the supplier. This doesn't include any of their internal email communication and meetings, nor does it include activities with other people from the client side (other than the key contact). This is to highlight that we cannot overlook the amount of effort the key contact needs to put in to making a deal like this happen.

Context: as is so often the case there had been many efforts over the years to try to sell to this particular country within the global network of organizations, both with partners and directly. However, there had been no active deal cycle for more than 12 months, and this key deal case study starts with a fresh sales team and a fresh conversation on the client side.

In an ideal world every account in your portfolio has a fully completed account plan, all key stakeholders mapped out, research and intelligence being conducted on a regular basis, the marketing team bringing leads of people that are interested and other leads coming in from other sources – life is good and things look rosy! However, in reality things are very different. You have a view of your accounts and an initial plan or strategy in place and while you are working on a 'best effort' basis to cover everything, your limited resources tend to naturally focus on where there is existing revenue that needs to be protected, or with confirmed opportunities. You often get around to deeper strategic planning when things are lighter and/or you need more pipeline. Therefore, there is often a catalyst that brings one of your prospect accounts into focus.

Cycle 1 – five months

Among the general sales and marketing prospecting activities for this account, the catalyst that started the new deal cycle (Cycle 1) came from a warm introduction. A new employee started at the supplier organization and as part of the general conversation when getting to know someone new, including a bit of background research, it became apparent that he used to work at one of the supplier's current key clients.

Step 1 (mapping of relationships): this person was leading business development for a specific vertical at a country level for this prospect. They were added to the current relationship map, along with the key data points and a guesstimate for their place within the org chart.

Step 2 (research and intelligence gathering): their role profile and social media was researched, and from talking to people it was possible to gain an understanding of the role, and its impact on the organization's objectives and how those link to the supplier's value proposition. The internal contact who knew them also provided an insight into their personality and the most suitable communication style.

Step 3 (engagement strategy): as part of their general catch-up activities with ex-colleagues the new internal contact had lunch with the ex-colleague. After discussion they were keen to explore further, so an introduction to the salesperson on that particular prospect account was made and he took the formal conversation forward.

STATUS AFTER CYCLE 1

After a couple of meetings, the value was recognized and they were keen to explore further, discussing it with their immediate line manager and others. Based on these internal conversations and guidance, they navigated a way around the various internal stakeholders to garner interest and support. After numerous back-and-forths a dead end was reached, and it was determined that moving forward would not be possible without support from the technology organization. This solution would touch a number of internal systems and would need to be owned and driven by someone in the technology organization, specifically CRM. The business team pushed for this, but there was no appetite to take the project on at that time. It wasn't a case of 'no' it was a case of 'not now', with support and appetite from someone in the CRM team needed to move forward.

Value from the three-step process: the initial entry into the account came from effective intelligence gathering (Step 2) to identify that a new internal employee on the supplier side had a good network of ex-colleagues. This led to identifying that this person knew a business development leader within the prospect. Crafting the right strategy to engage with them (Step 3) was also key. It started with the two ex-colleagues having an informal lunch (where they introduced the value proposition and garnered interest), which then led to a warm introduction to the salesperson on this prospect account.

Cycle 2 – five months (total time to that point being 10 months)

The two kept in contact during this time, including an invitation to a networking dinner attended by peers in the sector. But the real break came around six months after the initial meeting when someone joined the prospect at a senior position within the CRM department. In this case the person was from one of the supplier's smaller prospect accounts, and it was great news as they were a supporter. Indeed, it turned out that they had mentioned the supplier's solution as part of the interview process. While the supplier had tracked this movement, the new CRM lead and the business development lead met on the client side before the supplier could help connect the dots.

The initial meeting was positive with both parties keen to explore a path forward. With a business need identified previously through the business development lead and the technology owner supportive, the next step was aligning the solution to support the corporate objectives and in doing so getting executive sponsorship. So, a meeting between the chief marketing officer (CMO) and head of industries was planned.

Step 1 (mapping of relationships): the CMO and head of industries were identified and mapped within the country level org chart. As they were senior executives their peers in the other countries where the supplier had already sold were also identified and mapped.

Step 2 (research and intelligence gathering): a refresh of all the key stakeholders was completed to check for any role movements as well as any latest developments. From LinkedIn analysis the supplier found out that there were some existing relationships with the key people they worked with in other countries. The next meeting was crucial, so it was important to understand the personalities and preferred communication styles of the new executives involved in the next phase of the deal cycle. Accordingly, videos were watched and other insight gleaned from social media posts. There was support from those on the client side, so the supplier could tailor the communication style, presentation and interactions to cater to their needs and requirements and ensure that the underlying business priorities were addressed.

Step 3 (engagement strategy): the engagement strategy for the CMO and head of industries was again led by the two internal supports, and they were able to align the value proposition with the new executives and get the call diarized. A dry-run session took place before the meeting, and the formal meeting happened at the end of this cycle.

STATUS AFTER CYCLE 2
The CRM leader became the supplier's internal champion. The meeting itself went very well, with the CMO and head of industries recognizing the value proposition and the need within their business, and that it aligned to their corporate priorities. They said they wanted to talk to their peers within the other countries that had already deployed the supplier's solution. These names were shared and the supplier heard that these conversations were being set up in the background.

They also expressed the need to get their information security team engaged in the process, and there were cursory conversations about where the budget would come from. A formal proposal had not been submitted at this time but some ballpark numbers had been informally mentioned. However, the key part of making this deal real was getting an executive sponsor onboard and getting agreement from the country-level leadership to put a solution like this in place.

It later became apparent that there were some key internal organizational changes happening behind the scenes. This meant that although the supplier knew internal conversations were happening and was in regular contact with the CRM leader, movement on the deal slowed down for a number of months without much tangible progress.

Value from the three-step process: stakeholder mapping (Step 1) became very important as this opportunity started to open up. There were new people being introduced who were senior and influential. These executives wanted validation from their peers in other countries, so it was important to 'connect the dots' for them. This was crucial as it provided the internal validation that was needed to take the solution forward with the right amount of enthusiasm and determination.

Cycle 3 – 10 months (total to date being one year and eight months)

Once a public announcement had been made stating the new country-level structure, the supplier was able to openly discuss and understand what this meant. The new leader was the chief growth officer (CGO) who would be the executive sponsor and budget signer, and they supported the existing agenda. However, they had more vigour and focus on precisely where the supplier's solution would fit, so there was a business need and the supplier's solution supported solving this.

Step 1 (mapping of relationships): the impetus to move things forward was gaining momentum, with other key stakeholders coming into view including the information security and data privacy teams. At an individual level, the CRM leader involved their direct line manager who was overseeing the CRM over a wider geographical region as well as the new names from the reorganization at the leadership level. Even though this deal cycle had been open for nearly a year it was still quite single-threaded from the supplier side, with the account executive and a technical person engaged with the day-to-day operations. When mapping the relationships this weakness was often noted. There had also been a long-standing relationship between the supplier and a partner, a leading CRM provider, who was also the global CRM of choice for the prospect. So, these relationships had already been identified and mapped previously but extra focus and leverage was used to gain insight to help with positioning.

Step 2 (research and intelligence gathering): the CRM leader had explained that the new CGO was going to be the key to moving the deal to signature. Interestingly, as part of this step it was found out that the supplier had actually met the CGO some years prior when they were in a different role. These old email exchanges were found and reviewed, revealing that at that time they were supportive and had tried to help the supplier with further introductions. Efforts were also made to connect the dots with the CRM partner, both at a country level and at a global level as well as the usual refresh of research and intelligence gathering to support the next round of interactions.

Step 3 (engagement strategy): the engagement channel between the supplier and client was mainly through the CRM leader who, as the internal champion, was anchoring most of the discussions on the client side. This included acting as the de facto supplier representative to answer questions and explain the solution, working as a go between when more information was required from the supplier and teeing up and leading key internal conversations (that didn't include the supplier). It also involved organizing key meetings with the supplier that included other necessary parties, such as the data privacy team.

At this stage the CRM leader's direct line manager started to play a more active role in the day-to-day discussions and meetings. There was a regular line of communication open with the CRM leader, including in-person meetings, both informally and as part of organized events that the supplier was hosting. When they and their line manager were attending the formal events organized by the supplier, they were exposed to the supplier's client base and were encouraged to discuss and build relationships with others in their industry. They also had the opportunity to meet the supplier's leadership and key personnel from other parts of the supplier's business, such as product and customer success. This forged a stronger bond between the client and supplier and built more trust.

The line of communication via the partner was active and being leveraged. This was used at a country level and also used to align and support the partner with their own global strategy with this very important global client of the partner's. It was heard that there were discussions about rolling out the supplier's solution globally on the back of a successful country-level deployment, and this was all positive. There was also another engagement thread through a client of the supplier. A meeting between the CGO and one of the supplier's key clients permitted the opportunity for the CGO to ask about the value proposition of the supplier and hear informal feedback from someone they trusted. The supplier heard about this encounter (from their client) and it added to the positive momentum.

STATUS AFTER CYCLE 3

This combined effort resulted in significant achievements during Cycle 3. With the reorganization came mobilization that was driven by the CRM leader. Conversations on the client side started with the data privacy team, during which time the CRM leader was acting as the go between. This gave them a basic understanding and the first meeting was arranged between the supplier and the data privacy team. It was an open item that continued for around 12 months before this team formally approved the solution. The first formal proposal was subsequently submitted, and as part of the client's internal budgeting and approval process a joint business case was worked on during the final part of this cycle. This allowed the supplier to introduce another key person from their side who was a business value consultant. The business case was completed jointly with the client and using the client's template.

However, despite building up a good level of momentum the deal was again running out of steam. One thing was startlingly apparent in that despite a number of requests and efforts, they had yet to formally meet the sponsor and the person who would sign the agreement, i.e. the CGO. This was a cause for concern when mapping the key stakeholders and defining the strategy.

Value from the three-step process: this was that pivotal stage in any strategic deal when the client is going through their own internal process. The cogs are turning and as a supplier you need to be supporting in any way you can – but crucially you need to let them go through their process (and not get in the middle of it). This cycle was really about getting the internal approvals, firstly from the information security and data privacy teams but also getting the business case signed off, so it was the engagement strategy (Step 3) that made the difference. Through multi-threading the supplier brought in their own domain experts to work with the client, and where necessary to connect them to their peers for validation and cross-referencing.

Cycle 4 – nine months (total to date being two years and five months)

The supplier was sure that, as part of their ongoing internal discussion, the CRM leader and the wider team were delivering the value proposition to the CGO and other key stakeholders. However, the supplier knew that a key signal the deal was going to happen would be when there was a direct line of communication opened up with the CGO.

Step 1 (mapping of relationships): the key stakeholders were already identified and mapped, but the supplier noted that more needed to be done to build momentum so there was an effort to exploit any under-utilized relationships.

Step 2 (research and intelligence gathering): a refreshed cycle of research and intelligence gathering was conducted. This focused on conversations with key people who would promote the business value and immediate need of the proposed solution.

Step 3 (engagement strategy): there were two key stakeholders outside of the current relationship sphere who were in positions of power. A lunch meeting was planned with one and a virtual meeting with the other, both of which were successful in that they recognized the value and need, and agreed to support the case internally.

After some forethought the team leading the deal on the supplier side decided to reach out directly to the CGO who was very active on LinkedIn. The account executive's line manager chose to write to the CGO via a LinkedIn direct message. They were not connected, so as part of a connection request they mentioned that they were working with the CGO's team, and that the organization's CEO was planning a trip into town. They suggested a meeting to coincide with the trip, a suggestion that was well received, and a meeting was subsequently planned.

STATUS AFTER CYCLE 4

The supplier had broadened the relationship at the executive level and now had their CEO and global head of strategic accounts engaged. During this meeting the CGO laid out his thinking for how the deal could move forward, including possible deliverables and some broad timelines. The deliverables were worked on jointly with the supplier and core team on the client side. It was in the form of a socialization presentation to explain the value proposition to the management team to get their support for the board approval. Once completed it was shared with the CGO, who took this forward, obtained board approval and secured funding. The contracting and commercial process followed and resulted in the signed deal, which was around five months after the first meeting between the CEO of the supplier and the CGO at the client.

Value from the three-step process: it was the well-executed engagement strategy (Step 3) that was the turning point. The deal became 'real' during the meeting between the CEO and the CGO. That line of communication was now open, and it was active throughout the final stages of the deal.

What we've learned in this chapter

In this chapter we have learned the following four key things:

- The importance of relationship mapping in winning key deals.
- How to apply relationship maps in key deals.
- How it was implemented in an example.
- The significance of the internal champion.

What's coming next

The next chapter will follow a similar structure and flow to this one but will be applied to key projects.

8

Relationship maps applied to key projects

Introduction

MARK HOLDEN, COFORGE – CHIEF BUSINESS OFFICER:
BANKING AND FINANCIAL SERVICES (EUROPE)

Sometimes I think back over my career about the deals I have worked on: the intensity, the pressure and the all-consuming nature of those types of strategic pursuits. When it is finally over and we did all the right things and won, there is a sense of relief that the marathon is over. However, instead of rest and celebration it's the opposite in that the signing of the contract signals the start of the race for our client. All the hard work building enough trust for the client to award us the business now needs to be backed up with delivering the outcomes we promised. The sales process is 'talking the talk' and project delivery is 'walking the walk'.

In my experience with managing large portfolios of business, when you get the delivery and execution of the project right, growth in the form of more business undoubtedly follows. If you don't, then unfortunately all of the hard work during the sales process – which heightened expectations – may be wasted. This could lead to the relationship entering a valley of disillusionment for both the supplier and client. The supplier's time and resources are then taken up trying to get things back on track, the client is unhappy, there are escalations and in the end the reputation of the supplier can get damaged. Consequently, the client is left disappointed and, more importantly, without the outcomes that were agreed. So, any way I think about it I need to do everything within my power to ensure our delivery meets and exceeds the client's expectations.

To do this consistently there are four prerequisites. First is re-defining and agreeing the goals, objectives and milestones. These must be crystal clear; it is a critical success factor. Second, we need to have a robust, competent team who possess the skills and capabilities needed to deliver successfully and who are managed effectively. All too often I see clients bewildered that the team being assembled to take on delivery is less experienced or qualified than the team on display during the sales cycle. Getting this right gives confidence to the client and is central to a successful outcome.

Third, it goes without saying that risk management is a critical component of every delivery, and it is necessary to identify, monitor and control risk. Neglect any hazards at your own peril since projects that commence without adequately assessing the potential risks of complications will inevitably encounter failure. Finally, and probably most importantly, is communication, and miscommunication between the team and stakeholders can be disastrous. Therefore, open and transparent dialogue between all parties, preferably using a good project management platform, is essential. It is best summed up by a phrase I will always remember from my Infosys days: in God we trust, everyone else bring data.

What is a key project?

Key projects are defined in much the same spirit as key deals and it's fair to assume that any key deal you win becomes a key project. So, from the client's perspective these would be projects that have a transformative impact, provide market positioning and a competitive advantage, and grow revenue or reduce costs (or both). From the supplier's side they are strategically important, provide the opportunity to expand into a new market or sector, create a new offering or are with a strategic client. These projects would typically have a long-term impact on the supplier's business and involve the delivery of a complex solution.

The project will usually entail direct involvement of senior stakeholders from the client side and could have a material impact on their business. These stakeholders may be from the management team and will likely sit across various functions on the client side. The project will require collaboration and coordination among multiple departments, teams or external partners to ensure a successful outcome, so this will require extensive planning and resources from the supplier. Considering all of these factors it implies that there will be inherent risks, uncertainties and challenges while underpinning all of this will be the pressure of a set of defined timelines, milestones or deadlines. These probably feed into other dependencies, as this key project may be a critical piece to a wider strategic programme.

The hand-off between signing the deal and starting the project

Any of us that have been involved with winning key deals will resonate with the sense of relief that comes when the deal is finally signed and, naturally, there is celebration within the winning team and across the wider supplier organization. However, such work can be intense and protracted with high expectation that the deal will be coming and lots of wondering from people as to why it hasn't come yet; thus, when the decision is finally made it can be more a sense of relief than celebration. It can be likened to crossing the finish line after a gruelling cross-country trek with many peaks and troughs, but imagine if that trek happened to last 6–12 months (or even longer). Whatever the feeling there is an element of 'closure' to the process, but the reality is something very different, and from the client's perspective this is just the beginning of the relationship.

I'd like to ask you to think about what happens during the shift from winning a deal to starting the project. Figure 8.1 shows an illustration of what the activity trend of data between the supplier and client might look like, and the lull in activity is the timeframe between the end of deal cycle and the start of the project.

FIGURE 8.1 Activity trend between supplier and client over a three-month period

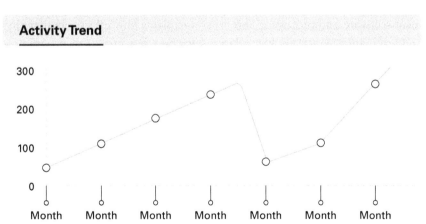

When people see this trend, they are usually very surprised to see the drop off in activity as soon as the deal is won. However, when you discuss what happens after the deal is closed and while the project is waiting to get started, they describe precisely what the figure shows, i.e. not much happening. If this is the case on your side, then it's something you should think about addressing immediately since 'buyer remorse' is a real thing. The client can feel at their most vulnerable after making a buying decision, and they often need immediate reassurance. Such action is important as goodwill, credibility and momentum can get lost, especially if stakeholder roles are changing. If you can, get ahead of this and form an understanding of who from your side and the supplier side will be involved in the project, and then get them introduced – or at least up to speed on the project prior to the deal being won. This comes back to identifying and mapping the key relationships, and then going through the research and intelligence-gathering phase before executing on the engagement strategy.

How to make a key project successful

This section highlights the core elements that are essential to making a project successful. These will be discussed in turn, and we'll highlight the significance of relationship quality for each point. Some of the data points and reference material links back to the insight from Chapter 2 where I presented the findings of my doctoral research.

Before we get into the details within this section, it's worthwhile noting that I've never taken any project management training or courses. This book isn't designed to explain anything about what specifically happens in a formal project management process, which often involves specialized project management software and processes. This section explains how effectively mapping and leveraging the stakeholder relationships on a key project or programme will significantly increase your chances of success. So, it will discuss the typical things to consider as part of key project, with a focus on the relationship aspect. These steps are not formal or fixed, nor do they have to be in this order, and in fact some are actioned in a different order or started in parallel.

Signing the deal

The first step here is the last step from the key deals chapter. While it's often the case that project teams will be getting ready prior to signing, including having conversations with the client, getting the contract signed is usually the official first step in starting the project. But the backstory to getting to this spot can sometimes have been a long one, often taking many months if not years. Therefore, it's important to complete a formal objective audit to get a clear perspective as to who from your side has a relationship with who from the client side.

If there have been some trust issues or poor communication during the sales cycle it might result in some hangover as the project starts. In addition, if the contract negotiations were contentious, perhaps leading to unfavourable terms from the client's perspective or them having the perception of not getting what they were promised, there could also be a bad ambience. Ideally, that isn't the case and there is a good relationship at this stage; one that fosters trust and transparency between both parties, ensuring clarity in the terms and conditions of the contract and the mutual obligations and objectives.

Effective communication

When we look back throughout this entire book, effective communication is one common thread that when done correctly offers every chance of a successful outcome; however, when there are problems it spells disaster. This is all about effective communication and I wanted to reiterate it. Establishing clear lines of communication includes all parties, such as team members, stakeholders and project sponsors, and it's imperative that open and honest dialogue is the norm. This helps build trust and facilitates the exchange of information. Opening discussions with the key stakeholders on the project's progress, including the challenges and milestones, ensures that everyone is on the same page and key people are kept informed and involved.

Poor communication can hinder a project's success as it can lead to gaps in information, misunderstandings, missed requirements and delays in addressing issues. Thus, it's crucial to establish robust communication channels to ensure that all key stakeholders are adequately informed. This avoids either leaving the client in the dark or them having the perception that key decisions are being made without their involvement. One way to avoid that is to actively seek feedback during the transition phase, especially at key junctures. Listen to their input and suggestions and try to incorporate their feedback to ensure that their objectives are considered and addressed.

The key part to this is a strong relationship map, as then you are able to tailor communication styles, channels and messages to suit stakeholder personality and preferences. This will increase engagement and their understanding which means they'll be more likely to provide comments and feedback, offer their support and generally contribute to problem solving, all of which increase the chances of project success.

Project kick-off meeting

After the deal is signed the first formal step that typically happens with the client is the project kick-off meeting. This is meant to align the teams, clarify objectives and any potential risks, and confirm the plan for what follows, the basis for this often being a project plan discussed during the sales process. This meeting acts as the bridge between the sales process to sign the deal and the team that will deliver the project. There would be a set of individuals working on the deal from both the client side and within your own organization, and during this process a lot of information would be shared and a lot of commitments made (contractually or otherwise).

All of this key information needs to have been captured and properly handed over as part of a transition process to the team delivering the project. Obviously, this includes detail on the key stakeholders too, with proper insight into each of them and an understanding of who from the client side will remain in place for the delivery of the project. It's important to work on a strategy in relation to who from your side will remain as part of the project team, or at least as part of the handoff. Ideally, there will be individuals from your side who were deliberately introduced as part of the deal cycle knowing they'll be key to delivering the project, so some of those relationships will already be in place.

Life is made so much easier when the project kick-off meeting has a friendly atmosphere, with familiar faces and with people having a clear expectation of what follows. So, a lot of this groundwork should be done as part of the sales process. Strong relationships here facilitate open communication and enable people to express ideas freely and collaborate as part of this new team. Nonetheless, be careful since any clashes of personality or strained relationships brought over from the sales process (or that become apparent early on in the project kick-off phase) can create conflicts and seriously hinder the success of the process.

Aligning to project objectives

We've spent quite a bit of time thus far highlighting the importance of clearly understanding and aligning to client objectives when it comes to building and maintaining high-quality relationships. The efforts to do this through the deal cycle get you to the point of winning the project, but this story continues with key projects. Perhaps unsurprisingly, strong stakeholder relationships are essential for defining clear project objectives and getting a comprehensive understanding of their needs, expectations and desired outcomes. This is crucial to the success of the project. Sitting at the heart of that is active involvement of the key stakeholders in objective-setting discussions, which will result in well-defined objectives that align with their corporate outcomes. It's only with this type of collaborative approach that stakeholders feel bought in and committed, and will in turn give their support to the project, thereby laying a solid foundation for project success.

There are a number of important things that need to be considered as part of aligning to project objectives, and it starts with **reaffirming the objectives** of the project. During the transition phase from the sales process to project delivery it's important to reaffirm your understanding of the client's needs, objectives and expectations. Be sure to seek clarification to ensure a shared understanding through identifying, mapping and engaging with the key stakeholders on the project. However, be mindful that some of them will be new. One issue to look out for when you shift from the sales process to project delivery is any sign of **overpromising** (or misunderstanding from the client side). If there is clear evidence that unrealistic promises have been made to the client during the sales process, now is the time to ensure this is brought to the surface internally on the supplier side. Then you can decide what action to take. It might be a case of having some difficult conversations with the client or adjusting things internally to ensure there are no serious issues early on in the relationship. Again, it's about communication and that includes your internal communication.

Having a **lack of clear objectives** is an issue. Without well-defined project objectives the team may lack direction and purpose and, more importantly, there will be no link to the real business benefits of the project. If this seems to be the case, it's worth challenging this with the stakeholders you are engaged with. Have some meaningful conversations and push your best practices for successful projects, and talk about the typical ways that you deliver value as the basis for the business benefits and return on investment conversation. Flowing from the objectives are the client's requirements which detail the functionalities, features, constraints and characteristics that the product or service must possess to meet the project objectives.

Inadequate requirement gathering will impact the success of the project because it will lead to incorrect assumptions about the client's needs. This may result in a solution that does not meet the client's expectations and which will impact the quality of the final outcome and the project's ability to deliver business value. However, strong stakeholder relationships will allow any misalignment or lack of clarity to be addressed and can be a catalyst for effective requirements gathering. Nonetheless, **shifting client priorities** within the organization or with the key stakeholders you are working with can impact upon the project's outcome. Changes in strategic direction or competing projects can redirect the attention of the key stakeholders supporting your project, which can result in client-side resources being moved around. Understandably this can lead to delays and affect the success of the project. The quality of your stakeholder relationships and the flow of information coming from them will, therefore, be key to providing any insight into whether any changes of direction are happening. These could be personnel changes or other events that may impact upon your project. If this is the case it's important for it to be recognized internally and measures taken to address it, even if it impacts upon your current project. This is because without the attention and support of key stakeholders it will be very hard to make the project a success.

One common issue on projects is **scope creep**. This refers to uncontrolled or undocumented changes in project scope, and it occurs when the project's scope expands beyond what was initially agreed upon with the client. Without proper change control processes in place additional requirements may be introduced, leading to delays and an increase in your costs if you are doing this without getting paid. If it's without the necessary formal approvals to deliver the additional scope this can also cause issues. But, by maintaining strong stakeholder relationships the project teams can foster open and regular communication with stakeholders to facilitate the early identification of potential scope changes or scope creep.

If the client is not willing to pay for these, then a strong person on the supplier side is required to push back against these requests. So, it works best to decide beforehand who will play that role and they can come in at the right time to have those conversations. However, considering some of the inputs from Chapter 2 it's not to say that you should create conflict with any type of reasonable request. Taking on board new things that might not have been considered previously but are now important to the client (and perhaps would have been considered or now that you know about them are actually useful ideas) can be a great way to build trust and cement the partnership. And remember, a partnership is a two-way street and you will likely need some leeway from the client at some point, so building up some goodwill is always a good approach.

In summary, the project objectives sit at the heart of a successful project and for the reasons discussed here things can go awry. But with a strong team in place and even stronger relationships, trust will be established and the client will feel confident in your ability to deliver the project successfully.

Allocation of the resources to deliver the project

Clients quite rightly believe that the quality of the people you assign to the project will have a direct correlation to the success of the project. This was supported by the insight from the interviews I conducted with executives that were summarized in Chapter 2, where they stated that it is one of the main components for a successful outcome. So, as efforts are made on your side to identify and assign the right team to make this project a success, it's important to bear in mind the mechanism by which you introduce these people to the client.

Each project is different and from the stakeholder side you can't be sure who will be on the project team from your side or the client's side until the project is kicking off. The case study in this chapter covers one example which involved the worldwide deployment of software for a global organization. By the time we got to the project kick-off after nine months of negotiating the deal almost everyone on the client side was completely new; in fact, on the project kick-off call they were asking what the software did and how it worked. Due to circumstances on the supplier side almost all were new to the project too. This was mainly due to people on both sides leaving the organization or moving to other internal roles, so it was probably a worst-case scenario from a stakeholder perspective. In such cases it's necessary to go back and refresh the relationship map from the deal, and then conduct another round of research and intelligence gathering to see who sits where and identify any gaps or people that have moved on.

When assembling your team try to include people who are familiar to the client team and the sales process; this will help to avoid the client getting frustrated that they are either repeating key information or correcting information. As was also explained in Chapter 2, it's very hard to overcome clashes of personality. One of the executives I interviewed explained that if there is a clash of personalities it's very difficult to get past that and maintain a good working relationship. So, where there are existing relationships try to be objective to detect any existing clashes and also take this into consideration when assembling the team, defining the roles and responsibilities and pairing them with people from the client side.

One key piece to this jigsaw is having **strong leadership** in place from the supplier side. This means appointing a competent project leadership team who are able to articulate a clear vision and have the ability to motivate and inspire the team. Capable leaders will provide direction, make informed decisions, set realistic expectations and resolve conflicts to keep the project on track. The importance of this should have become apparent in the 'aligning to project objectives' section where we discussed the tough conversations that may need to happen with regard to issues around a lack of clear objectives, inadequate requirements gathering, shifting client priorities and scope creep. If any of these things start to happen then it's important that those tough conversations are had as soon as possible, and having strong stakeholder relationships will enhance the effectiveness of your leadership. Mapping these relationships allows the leaders to step in with ease when required and effectively influence and mobilize support from key stakeholders on the client side.

Along with the strong leadership it's important to have a **skilled team**. As such, assembling a skilled and capable project team with the necessary expertise and competencies to deliver a successful project is central to a positive outcome. When looking at the team you are assembling to deliver the project some honest and objective assessments need to be made. In an ideal world you would have the strongest team possible, but as anyone that has been doing this for a while can attest, that is seldom the case. There will be those who are new to your organization or lacking experience, those who struggle to communicate effectively, those who have difficult personalities or other issues and those who are simply not very competent. But you will need to go with the best you have at that moment in time, and the key is knowing your potential weaknesses ahead of time. Ideally, you will be able to discuss this with others in the team and plan accordingly, potentially using external partners or contractors if required.

As the project moves forward, having strong stakeholder relationships on the client side can allow you to head off any concerns – such as lack of experience – prior to the team becoming engaged. They can also help you to detect any sense that the client isn't pleased or is ill at ease with whoever you have placed within the project team. Getting to the heart of these concerns and addressing them as soon as possible is very important.

Review and finalize the joint project plan and scope

Now the teams on both sides are getting established, one of the most important things to formalize is the project plan and the scope of the project.

During the sales process this often isn't done to the right level of detail, or things weren't discussed in the real-world scenario of the 'right here right now'. At this stage it's even more important that there is a feeling of open and honest communication.

This involves developing and agreeing upon a **comprehensive joint project plan**, one that outlines the objectives, scope, timeline, budget, resources and dependencies in enough depth that all parties are clear about what lies ahead. Emphasis is on the word 'joint' since it's something that both parties agree upon. This plan should serve as a roadmap for a successful project execution. Strong stakeholder relationships significantly contribute to robust project planning, as with open lines of communication their input and feedback can be captured. Client stakeholders often provide valuable insights regarding new risks, requirements and constraints that may be either here or on the horizon.

At this point there has been a project kick-off call, you are putting together the team to deliver the project and now you are agreeing on the project plan and scope, so now is the perfect time to objectively **assess the stakeholder engagement** from the client side. The central purpose of this book is to identify, map and develop key stakeholder relationships and the premise is that without the support of key stakeholders it will be very difficult to be successful. Therefore, you constantly need to be assessing the engagement from stakeholders. You don't always need to be in constant direct communication with these stakeholders as sometimes their points of view and feedback get channelled back via people from the client side, and if that is the case then you need to make an assessment as to the reliability of that information. But nevertheless, at this stage it's crucial that you have an understanding of who the right people are and that they are adequately engaged in the project. If they aren't then it's the time to raise the alarm internally.

Implementation, testing and full rollout of solution

The project is physically starting now with the implementation and initial **testing** (usually on a smaller group), and as each of these stages progress the seriousness of the decisions and acuteness of the impact become more and more prevalent. The common theme that you will see throughout all these steps is open and honest communication. As the development and initial testing is being done it's crucial that critical feedback is shared from the client side. As such, the quality of the relationships you have with the core client project team and, in turn, their relationships with the user acceptance testers and other people involved in the process will determine the success of this step and indeed the success of the wider project.

Depending on the size and scale of the project the **end-to-end rollout** of the solution can take weeks, months or years to complete. It's about deploying the final product or service in the client's environment and then giving access to the user base as well as end-user training. This step is really what 'the project' actually is. So, if there is a resistance or a lack of cooperation it will likely impede the deployment process, which can lead to delays or could even derail the project. If there are issues, it's probably because there are some strained relationships somewhere in the mix. At this stage it's a good time to go through the relationship-mapping process from Part 2 to ensure you have the full picture. Positive, trusting relationships will ensure a collaborative deployment process and increase the chances of a smooth rollout.

All of the steps discussed are important but if I had to pinpoint one place in particular that I see things fail it's the **client's internal communications**. This is the start of the change management piece and as with anything new (technology solution or otherwise), its impact is muted if people don't adopt it. From what I've witnessed, when the benefits – or why they should care – are effectively communicated to those who need to make the change, it offers the best chance of success. Ideally, this message should be delivered by someone senior or a figurehead who believes in what they are saying and is 'walking the walk' as well.

It's crucial that this stage goes well, and from a relationship perspective the supplier needs to be stronger in their assertions with regard to what they have seen work and what they have seen fail. This might mean having some hard conversations about how the client is planning to communicate with those impacted by the solution. This stage can sometimes be run entirely by the client, but the supplier has to be involved and share their best practices. If this step isn't a success then while the project might be a technical success, the business users may not all adopt it, and thus may not get the full value. The consequence of such a scenario is the project not delivering the business outcomes it promised.

Remember that as the rollout is happening there is also a review and **feedback loop**. In most cases this will be 'live', so anything useful can be incorporated into the ongoing rollout or else it can be captured for changes and updates later. The stakeholders involved in and connected to the end users are the ones who will be able to collect this feedback, so focus on these individuals and enable them to be aware of the significance of the feedback. Notably, it will be the quality of your relationship with them that will allow you to get a view into this feedback loop. But crucially, it's the quality of their relationship with the end users as well as how engaged they are (as a result of the proper communication plan) that will determine their motivation to give honest feedback.

Thinking back to Chapter 2 again, two things that were emphasized as being important in building trust as part of project delivery were the supplier being flexible and able to move with the needs of the business, and them being transparent and taking ownership of problems as they arise. As is so often the case 'things happen', so **being flexible and adaptable** to changes and unforeseen challenges that arise during the project is critical. This agile mindset will allow you to quickly respond to changing circumstances and adjust plans as needed. Having robust **quality control measures** will ensure that the project meets or exceeds the key stakeholders' expectations. Engaging them in the process to define the quality standards and acceptance criteria will ensure alignment between the project team's understanding of quality, and the stakeholders' expectations. This regular feedback loop enables the team to make necessary adjustments and course corrections.

It's important to proactively identify and assess **project risks**. Engaging key stakeholders in risk identification and analysis processes allows for a broader perspective on risks and their potential impact. Establishing **KPIs** to measure project progress and success is a key method to monitor and track performance. By involving stakeholders in the establishment of KPIs and metrics, the project team ensures that performance measures are meaningful and aligned with stakeholder expectations. Regularly sharing progress updates and performance reports with stakeholders enhances transparency and fosters accountability. All of this effort is ultimately put into place to **deliver business value**, so throughout the project it's important to capture the value that the project is delivering to the client as it happens. This involves reiterating how the project aligns with their goals and how it will address their specific needs.

Project closure

As the project ends and is handed over to the team providing the **ongoing support,** there is another transition of people in and people out from both the client and supplier side. Some will stay and some new ones will have been introduced at different stages of the project. Whatever the case, this provides another formal checkpoint at which to do a relationship audit and another cycle of what we discussed in Part 2. A review of the relationships will permit another objective assessment of the quality of relationships. Just as good relationships are helpful, poor relationships will hinder knowledge transfer or ongoing support which can lead to difficulties in the handover process or inadequate assistance post-project completion.

There needs to be a culture of **continuous improvement** through learning from past projects and applying lessons learned to future ones. By encouraging feedback, conducting post-project reviews and capturing best practices to enhance future project performance you will be in a position to make each project more and more of a success. Engaging stakeholders in post-project reviews and lessons learned exercises allows the project team to gather valuable insights and perspectives. Identifying successes, challenges and areas for improvement subsequently enables the team to implement targeted actions and initiatives. Critical to the success of such exercises are strong relationships, as these will encourage stakeholders to share their observations, recommendations and innovative ideas for future projects.

The importance of the internal champion(s)

Internal relationships are important across all three use cases, but I've made the point to call it out within the key projects use case as here it is really a make-or-break situation. Taking into consideration all the points we highlighted as being required to make a project successful, if you are starting a new project at a new account then having people on the client side to help you navigate your way around the organization is imperative. Whether it's just one person or you are fortunate enough to have more than one, having someone with a vested interest in making your project a success is key. This isn't just because someone has assigned them as the project manager, but ideally because they personally and firmly believe in the project, and potentially see it as a pathway for career progression and accolades.

This person will be required to do a huge amount of work, primarily the planning and organizing work needed to make any new project a success. It's especially true when you need to mobilize different teams on the client side to support and get involved in the project. You will need to be introduced to these new people and get them excited and onboard. For this to be effective it needs to be orchestrated by someone internally, and in my experience the success of the project is determined by the success of this role.

Summary of examples for mapping existing relationships for key projects

Plug the gaps across the key stakeholder landscape: when the initial relationship map of key stakeholders on the project is created it will become apparent where there are existing relationships and where there are gaps. Note here that you will likely have the relationship map from the deal cycle as the base. So, as you start to formulate your strategy to make the project a success, the depth and breadth of the map deepens and widens. Thus, it will become clearer where the gaps are based on current relationships as well as the ones you will need to make for the project to succeed.

Uncover existing unknown relationships to support the project: identifying relationships that you are unaware of will aid the project. This is especially true if they are key stakeholder relationships that can have an impact on the project. Thus, identifying, mapping and developing a pathway to those stakeholders forms part of the overarching strategy to support the project's success.

Monitor and strategize around key stakeholder engagement throughout the project: I'd argue that a relationship map is the central document used as part of the strategy to be successful, whether for a key deal, key project or key account. Defining and tracking the actual engagement against the strategy will help keep you on course. Using it as part of your conversations with the client (especially the client champion) will help you to articulate your vision as part of the joint project plan and get them onboard. If they understand what is needed from a relationship perspective to make the project a success, they'll buy in and will be better armed to facilitate.

Case study 2: Global consulting and systems integrator

Client: a global organization, with over 250,000 employees and generating more than $10 billion in annual revenue.

Supplier: SaaS organization selling enterprise software.

Deal scope: a nine-month pilot project was initially sold and is the focus of this case study. An enterprise deal was positioned during the pilot phase, and the value of the enterprise deal was in the top 10 of all deals closed in the organization's history (having been established for more than 10 years).

Timeline: the pilot project itself was timed to last nine months, but as you will read there were some issues during that process. Consequently, the timeline from signing the pilot contract to completion was 22 months, and therefore, this is the timeframe of this case study.

Relationship capital invested: this section is to highlight the amount of time that was put into this process by the key contact on the client side (who in this case was not the champion but the project manager). The volume of activities was split over two people and the total timeframe of this project was two years and 11 months. The key contacts exchanged just under **2,000 emails** and attended more than **250 meetings** with the supplier. This does not include any of their internal email communication and meetings, nor does it include activities with other people from the client side (other than the key contact). This is to highlight that we cannot overlook the amount of effort the key contact needs to put in to support such a project.

Context: the deal cycle to sell the pilot project took more than 15 months, and by the time it was finally signed the key stakeholders from the client side had moved on. The same was true on the supplier side with both the account executive and their manager leaving (the latter being the executive that helped to get the pilot deal agreed).

Cycle 1 – eight months

This case study starts from the project kick-off call. As a result of all the changes in personnel on the client side, while those on the call understood the overall business outcomes that were expected there was a lack of clarity from them on what the software actually did and how it worked. Also, it turned out that some key internal approvals had not been given on the client side, so those approval cycles needed to happen before the project could start.

Step 1 (mapping of relationships): all but one of the key stakeholders from the deal cycle had left the client by the time the deal was signed. The one who remained was the global lead for sales operations and the executive sponsor of the project. So, of the five people from the client side that were on the project kick-off call, four were completely new and had no knowledge of the supplier or what the software did. These included the technical owner of the software, the project manager and technical and business support. These stakeholders were identified and mapped into the org chart along with other names that came up during these early conversations.

Step 2 (research and intelligence gathering): the desktop research uncovered some financial performance issues and quite significant attrition issues.

This insight was gathered from published articles and supplier experience, and through the intelligence-gathering process it was established that there didn't seem to be a high level of morale.

Step 3 (engagement strategy): the anchor person from the supplier side was the Customer Success Manager (CSM) who was new to the team, so efforts were needed to build credibility and trust. This person was responsible for managing the 'day-to-day' of the account. There was also an account executive who maintains the role of the account manager. Access to stakeholders is a lot easier when there is a formal project being rolled out, and it's very different to a sales cycle. This is because there are diarized meetings that have specific agenda items with people from the client side who are formally assigned to the project and have things that they need to deliver on. So, those communication channels are open and through the cycle of diarized and ad hoc calls, the momentum builds.

STATUS AFTER CYCLE 1

Unfortunately, the project didn't start as expected. While the initial software install happened without major incident, the approvals for the users of the software were not in place and took around six months to be implemented following the project kick-off call. Considering that almost the whole team was new when the project started, there was more personnel turnover during Cycle 1. During this time, two key people from the project as well as the technical owner of the software and the project manager left from the client side. Their two replacements joined the team and during Cycle 1 some other key stakeholders were presented to, including the CMO for the Americas and the global lead for strategic accounts. There were also a few other key people on the project team. By the end of Cycle 1 a new project team was in place, the software was installed and the users were onboarded' although this had taken six months compared to what would usually be one to two months.

Value from the three-step process: considering all of the changes in personnel on the client side, especially when the project was just starting, the core value came from the mapping of stakeholders (Step 1) and the research and intelligence gathering (Step 2).

Cycle 2 – 18 months (total to date being two years and two months)

The pilot was contracted to last nine months; however, it was already seven months into the pilot by the time the users were onboarded. Through discussion between the supplier and client there was subsequently an agreement to extend the pilot for a further six months until just after the end of Cycle 2. The way the software works is that after the initial install and processing of user data there is an output that showcases the insight derived, and it's used to scope out the opportunity and path forward. As part of the agreement to extend the pilot an enterprise-wide proposal was shared. This was supported by a business case which was underpinned by specific scenarios that would deliver the business value and return on investment. These scenarios were the key to Cycle 2 as they linked to specific roles within the client organization.

All these things culminated in a key in-person executive meeting. The purpose of this was to recap on the insights captured so far, present the opportunity and route to value and, crucially, to agree on what would be the most valuable and easily executable projects to deliver during the pilot. This would, in turn, prove (or disprove) the business case. The ultimate objective of these projects was for the senior business leaders anchoring each project to acknowledge that value was delivered. The desired outcome was for them to support the case for adopting the software more widely, thus leading to the agreement of the enterprise proposal. The executive meeting went well and a solid plan of action was agreed.

Step 1 (mapping of relationships): the current key stakeholders were already mapped; however, the discussion on which mini projects to choose resulted in four that were of particular interest. Other new stakeholders were introduced, including the global lead for all go-to-market activities. The partner ecosystem was also engaged through collaborating with the client's CRM provider, and someone was assigned from the client to get feedback from the end users (which was crucial). In this project one mini project was from marketing, so it needed someone from marketing to anchor. One was merger and acquisitions, so it needed to work with an organization the client had acquired; one was a new business mini project, so it needed someone from the new business/prospecting team; and the final one was an alliances mini project, so it needed to work with the alliances team. Each mini project needed a senior executive to sponsor it, and then an assigned team to support the development and execution. Thus, mapping was done to identify potential candidates across all of these areas.

Step 2 (research and intelligence gathering): the organizational-level research and intelligence gathering was still producing similar insights on the performance and attrition issues. When applied to the stakeholder level it helped to decide which stakeholders to approach as part of the use-case-planning process. Who to approach was discussed and agreed in collaboration with the champion on the client side, who was also the project manager.

Step 3 (engagement strategy): there were what could be described as the 'business as usual' diarized and ad hoc meetings (as well as email exchanges and calls), including virtual and in-person meetings. The in-person meetings comprised formal business meetings and informal lunches/drinks as well as inviting key personnel to peer-to-peer networking events. These things were happening, but here we'll focus specifically on the mini projects. Core to the success was the project manager from the client side who was a real believer in the software and that it could support the overall business outcomes. Indeed, their professionalism and dedication were the key to taking this forward, and the supplier worked directly with them every step of the way. From initially identifying the potential executives to approach, they then helped with mapping them into the correct place within the organization. The initial emails were drafted in collaboration and the project manager sent them out and, where required, also followed up with internal chats and phone calls. Often a meeting was needed – which they handled – and for which preparation was done in advance. If there were replies they weren't sure about how to handle, they were again discussed together and responses drafted collaboratively.

STATUS AFTER CYCLE 2

There was attrition on the supplier side this time, with the CSM moving on to a different organization. However, this was covered as the account executive from the supplier side was well connected to the project manager and wider team from the client side. Thus, the transition to the new CSM happened quite well but engagement with the executives for the four mini projects resulted in mixed success. Two gave their full commitment and engaged their team to work on these projects, but while the other two accepted that there was value they were slow to engage their team.

Value from the three-step process: this phase was about building relationships with the teams on the client side that would anchor the mini projects. So, managing the engagement strategy (Step 3) was the key. This was driven by the internal champion who was instrumental to making it happen.

Cycle 3 – nine months (total to date being two years and 11 months)

At the beginning of Cycle 3 the end of the extended pilot was fast approaching. Attrition remained a problem with two of those driving the mini projects having moved out from the client organization. In addition, the organization's margin and growth rates were under pressure which resulted in keyboard-level changes. Consequently, there was a lot of flux within the client organization, coupled with budget freezes and the fact that the four mini projects had not completed their natural gestation period. Therefore, it became apparent that positioning the enterprise deal for a signature in September (including the approval process) wasn't going to happen.

The decision was jointly made to stop delivering the service towards the middle of Cycle 3 but to continue working together to find a pathway to an enterprise deal. This included working on an updated business case, incorporating feedback and datapoints, and on the plus side it gave a bit more time to work on the outcomes from the mini projects.

Step 1 (mapping of relationships): keeping the map up to date based on the attrition was hard to manage, but the main stakeholders were captured and tracked.

Step 2 (research and intelligence gathering): the key people the supplier was working with were clearly identified, and through regular conversations it was evident that there was trepidation. From research and intelligence gathering it was clear that people from senior management and other key roles were either moving roles or moving out of the organization completely, and there was a bar on all spending (including business travel).

Step 3 (engagement strategy): this was the final stage of the pilot and there was a push towards the decision, but it was clear that this wasn't on a positive track.

STATUS AFTER CYCLE 3

With hindsight it's easy to see that the likelihood of an enterprise agreement happening wasn't high. However, at the time the process was followed with full commitment from the supplier side and the key stakeholders, including the original executive sponsor, were telling the supplier that they were overwhelmingly in agreement on the value the solution would deliver. Nonetheless, when it came to action they were unwilling or unable to force a conversation to get the budgets approved at that time. Thus, there was an acknowledgement to the old adage of the relationship break-up in those discussions of 'it's not you, it's us'.

The conversations about the enterprise agreement extended towards the end of Cycle 3. During that time the original executive sponsor also left the client organization, as did two other key people from the core team.

Value from the three-step process: as you have gathered, the thread running throughout this case study was the changes in personnel, so getting ahead of that and being able to adjust their expectations based on what was happening on the client side helped. The ongoing mapping of stakeholders (Step 1) and research and intelligence gathering (Step 2) were core to this.

Concluding comments

I was debating whether to use this case study or not as it's not a happy ending, but I'm a strong believer that you do learn more from failures than successes. As you just reviewed the section called 'what makes a key project successful' there were warning signs, and as these signs were heeded on the supplier side there was an acceptance that the deal was very unlikely. But the important part I wanted to highlight within this case study was the impact of the internal champion. The project manager who orchestrated the engagement for the four mini projects was crucial to giving this pilot any chance of success. And while it didn't end as planned, the conversations are still open with this client to the day of writing this book, and it's not a question of 'no', it's 'not now'. However, the learnings are crucial and warranted inclusion. The positives of the relationship mapping, such as identifying these problems identified early on, helped the supplier to minimize the losses and keep the relationship on track for the future so that some rewards might be realized in the long term.

The difference between a key deal and a key project (and in this case a pilot) is that the project has to deliver the actual value, whereas with a key deal the client needs to be convinced that the solution will deliver the value. But to achieve this there are a multitude of things that need to happen on the client side to lead to a successful outcome, and if some key things don't happen then the project's success is severely hindered. Recognizing these signs and making moves to avert any issues is the learning, and sitting central to mitigating any of this risk is a properly executed relationship map.

What we've learned in this chapter

We have learned the following four key things:

- The importance of relationship mapping in delivering key projects.
- How to apply relationship maps in key projects.
- How it was implemented in an example.
- The significance of the internal champion.

What's coming next

So far in Part 3 we have learned how to apply relationship maps in key deals and key projects, and the next chapter will bring this together as applied to managing key accounts.

9

Relationship maps applied to key account management

Introduction

DR HEIDI K. GARDNER AND IVAN MATVIAK, CO-AUTHORS OF THE BESTSELLING BOOK *SMARTER COLLABORATION: A NEW APPROACH TO BREAKING DOWN BARRIERS AND TRANSFORMING WORK*

Smarter, deliberate collaboration within one's organization as well as with clients and other third parties generates appreciably higher revenue and profits compared to siloed or less intentional ways of working. Our work, originally at Harvard and now with thousands of senior executives worldwide, consistently demonstrates these outcomes. It doesn't matter about the sector, organization size or region; in all cases the combined strength of the right collaborators generates major value (see Figure 9.1).

For example, within the highest-performing branches of a global retail bank, different kinds of bankers craft higher-quality, integrated offerings for customers. Frontline bankers link data, personal interfaces and targeted outreach to determine customers' needs and spark interest in the bank's products. Product specialists then meld these insights with their expertise to develop higher-value, customized offerings.

The more collaborative branches earned significantly higher revenue with this particular product *as well as* greater customer loyalty. This is because a broader and more targeted range of contributors thoughtfully engaged with customers and produced the following:

- More comprehensive and groundbreaking solutions to simplify customer experience.
- A positive image of the bank as a collaborative provider.
- Greater trust between the bank and customers.

FIGURE 9.1 Financial benefits of smarter collaboration[21]

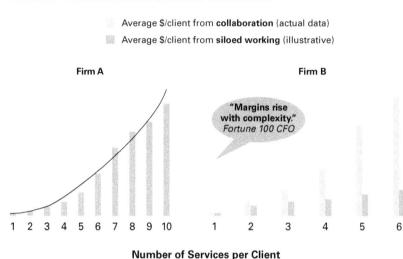

Smarter collaboration may lead to one-off projects or products. But the most lucrative opportunities result from starting with a complex customer (or client) challenge or opportunity; dissecting it to figure out exactly who should be working on it when, and for what inputs; and tackling the issue accordingly. This leads to innovative, multi-pronged results.

Through addressing the bigger, more complicated challenges you gain access to higher-level executives who have larger responsibilities, bigger budgets and more sophisticated needs. You grow your reputation and reach within the client organization which sets you up for more sales. As you start working with more senior individuals (especially in the C-suite), your work becomes more valuable and has a higher margin. In addition, growing your relationship with existing clients costs less than capturing business with new clients.

We saw this phenomenon at work in a software organization which tracks the effectiveness of marketing campaigns. Most of their customers used another's data visualization software so that patterns in the data were easier to spot. However, applying this add-on was cumbersome. The software organization introduced their own data visualization tool which was easily integrated into their tracking package. The new tool was easy to use and came with reports and graphs directly tied to the marketing data. Consequently, they could charge more than competing products in the market, and the cost of sales was low because they were selling mostly to existing customers.

Since smarter collaboration involves starting with the end in mind such as understanding top goals, complex challenges and opportunities, it often means focusing on the most strategic client accounts. For example, it commonly entails spending more effort on companies that contribute the most revenue and have the largest potential for growth. To best serve these accounts, effective internal collaboration is crucial, and this includes:

- Identifying the right mix of experts and viewpoints to tackle their top challenges.
- Leveraging different forms of diversity, including people with different collaborative attributes, as revealed by the Smarter Collaboration Profile[22] psychometric tool.
- Creating an environment of trust in which all voices are heard, and task conflict is embraced.

When these ingredients are in place, collaboration produces much more innovative solutions for key account clients and prospects, thus allowing them to achieve their strategic objectives and prompting them to do more business with you. And by relationship mapping and appropriately engaging, as Dr O'Sullivan explores in this chapter, you further boost your highest-value business opportunities.

What is key account management?

The Pareto Principle,[23] also known as the 80/20 rule, tells us that roughly 80 per cent of outcomes are derived from 20 per cent of inputs. In revenue terms it would suggest that 80 per cent of an organization's revenue comes from 20 per cent of their clients. I raised this point during a conversation with a top executive at a global organization and they suggested, half joking and half serious, that actually 99 per cent of their revenue comes from just 1 per cent of their clients. I say half joking because they were referring to the fact there were over 100,000 'clients' in their CRM system, so 1 per cent of that number would be around 1,000 and perhaps the top 1,000 clients would be close to 99 per cent of the total revenue. But they were actually making a subtle joke about the fact that the vast proportion of the 100,000 clients would not be what you would call 'active'. Nevertheless, however you define a client – whether it's 80/20 or 99/01 – the point is that a huge amount of revenue comes from a very small number of clients. So, logic tells us that it makes sense to direct a disproportionate amount of focus to the accounts that contribute the most revenue and within those, the ones that have the largest potential for growth.

Key account management (KAM) is when there is a specific focus on managing and nurturing relationships with the most valuable clients. As the name suggests, these accounts are often referred to as key accounts but can also be known as strategic accounts and organizations may also have their own internal term to describe this set of accounts. This book uses the term 'key accounts'. When it comes to defining what constitutes a key account, as described above, the amount of **revenue** they generate is the key metric. Nonetheless, you might identify an account that has high **revenue potential** as being a key account. This might mean they don't currently generate a significant amount (or it may be the case that they are a prospect and not a client), but you want to place a special focus on them because you believe there is great potential. There may also be a scenario where a large account by revenue is simply too large to lose. The gap in revenue would create a huge burden on the supplier, so they become de facto 'key accounts'.

It might be decided that a specific organization is of **strategic importance**. This could be based on the sector or region in which it operates, and the supplier deems this client to be crucial to their success. Sometimes, a client will enter into a **long-term partnership** and these might involve a commitment to innovation or significant process improvements, or to the co-creation of a joint solution. The main point is that these relationships are different from the others. There are whole books written on KAM, but this chapter is designed to supplement the existing content and to have a special focus on the impact of identifying, mapping and developing existing relationships.

Such accounts are more complex than other types of accounts, which may include smaller customers, one-time purchasers or more transactional relationships. These other accounts are still important, but they'd typically be managed through a different approach. The distinction between key accounts and the rest lies in the level of resources, attention and focus dedicated to managing and growing them. The aim of KAM is to maximize the value derived from these accounts by providing exceptional service and personalized solutions as well as building long-term relationships. It is worth noting that key accounts are often the costliest to serve and can be less profitable than others. Managing a key account involves spending more time on fewer accounts, or in many cases having a dedicated key account manager and a multi-functional key account team, who all work on only one key account. This allows you to devote time to adequately cover the points highlighted in Part 2.

Selling to existing clients versus new clients

Considering that key accounts generate a significant amount of an organization's total revenue, the good news is that selling to an existing client is easier (faster, larger deals and more open to buy multiple service lines) than selling to a prospective client. This was discussed towards the end of Chapter 3. Over time you will have gained a good understanding of **client priorities** with existing clients and will already have that critical base level of knowledge. As such, there is already a sense of familiarity and, hopefully, a good level of **rapport and trust** has already been built. As part of this, **channels of communication** are already in place, so you know who to talk to for what and what internal processes to follow. It is important to remember that clients will incur switching costs if they change supplier. Customer retention depends on a good relationship between the supplier and the customer being sustained over time. If the supplier becomes complacent the customer will find a way to justify switching costs.

Depending on the industry, for example in consulting and IT services, supplier-client relationships can be so integrated that it is common for incumbent suppliers to work from a client email domain. They may also have access to their internal systems for things like organizational contact details and internal messaging applications as well as the ability to book meeting rooms. Once you start a solid conversation at a key account you can evidence a **proven track record** which includes pointing to successful projects and, most importantly, having a network of internal relationships that will vouch for you. Thus, there is a sense of **brand loyalty**. This should all lead to a **higher probability of selling** and a **quicker sales process** as there is less of a need to prove all the aspects just discussed. This is because, guess what, you already have a set of strong existing relationships. To get to this level can take months and more often years to achieve, but not having to go through all that **reduces the overall cost of sales and marketing**.

How to grow a key account

The growth of an account comes from winning deals, which was the subject of Chapter 7. Once you have won a deal you then need to deliver that project successfully, which was covered in Chapter 8. So while this chapter explores how to grow key accounts, it's working on the assumption that the core way that accounts grow is by winning deals and delivering those projects successfully, and then winning more deals and delivering those projects. Thus, that cycle continues. The elements to achieve this – as discussed in detail in those chapters – all hold true here, and I don't feel the need to repeat them all again. However, I'll reference some of the key ones that have a slightly different twist in the KAM context.

The intention of having more of a focus on a specific set of accounts is that you can devote more time to them and really focus on building trusted, meaningful relationships with the stakeholders that matter. Therefore, this section will discuss some of the items that are important components of a successful KAM strategy.

Key account identification

Identifying which accounts should be key accounts is central to making the key accounts initiative a success. Some of the typical criteria were mentioned in the last section, but a thorough analysis should be conducted to create a definitive final list which may also include others that are under consideration. These accounts can be compared by business model, their stated objectives, the industry and organizational-level challenges, and the opportunity. They can then be segmented based on their needs, revenue potential and other relevant criteria to develop a matrix to make objective decisions on which ones to include. And of course, an important input is the volume and quality of existing relationships, which will be discussed shortly.

This is also a two-way street, so if the client recognizes your organization as being strategic to their business too, this becomes a mutual agreement. Be cautious about treating them as a key account if they do not see you as a strategic supplier. In this case they could be a prospective key account, which requires further work for them to realize your potential as a supplier. Or they could simply be willing to sustain the relationship with you but are not interested in strategic projects.

Account planning

I've talked about the additional investment of time and resources for effective KAM, and this starts with developing a comprehensive account plan. It links back to some of the things discussed around the priorities and objectives of the key account. The account plan should start by analysing the customer's needs in depth and linking these needs to your organization's capabilities. Next you can outline the strategies, actions and initiatives required to drive growth, and these insights will only come with a deep understanding of the customer's business and their sector. You will then be able to address the identified challenges (typically underpinned by your organization's offerings), and it should include a plan to demonstrate the value you can deliver to the key account. Having this base level of knowledge from a thorough research and intelligence-gathering cycle will put you in the best position to be perceived as credible by the client, and will help you to build trusting relationships.

Building a relationship map

I have seen so many key account plans with just a cursory contact map – this book is an effort to fill that gap. Consider you have two very similar accounts with regard to organizational size, challenges, scale of the opportunity and the amount of revenue you generate from them. For one of them you have a strong set of existing executive-level relationships along with other key relationships, and for the other account the relationships are centred in one part of the business and are not strategic relationships.

Hopefully, it's easy to recognize that everything that needs to happen to be successful with winning key deals, making key projects successful and ultimately growing key accounts is easier, faster and more effective when you have existing relationships to leverage. At the very least, for research and intelligence gathering and then relationships directly with the C-suite and key stakeholders, everything works better when these relationships already exist.

There is a different amount of rigour involved when it comes to following the relationship-mapping process outlined in Part 2 for key accounts versus for key deals and key projects. Not least as the process of identifying, mapping and developing these relationships is an ongoing process, ideally lasting for many years. As outlined in the first step of the process in Part 2, identifying the key stakeholders and mapping them against the client's organizational structure should happen as soon as possible. And as you are focusing strategically on this account, the depth and breadth of contacts and relationships within a key account are critical to sustaining a high share of the client's spend over time.

The basic things are to map the management/executive team which, as already discussed, are usually published on the organization's website or else the key roles are usually easy to populate using LinkedIn searches. However, go further by understanding who the **business unit heads** are, both globally and regionally (do the regional heads report to the global head?). Often, you might find that there are also **regional heads** who are responsible for a specific geographical market. This may or may not include all business units, and sometimes the organization might break off a smaller region and handle that one differently to the others.

Try to find out who leads the **central functions** (HR, finance, IT, sales and marketing, etc) and where the key people are located. When you delve into the offerings the client has you will understand their horizontal service lines, which are the things they sell to clients. Again, each will likely have a global lead and a regional lead. A lot has been discussed about the significance of your **internal champions**, so mapping where they fit is important, as is identifying and mapping **adversaries** or people aligned to competitors. As you have read through the case studies in Chapters 7 and 8, and the ones that follow in Chapter 9, it will become apparent that the internal champion is often the most crucial component to any deal, project or account.

The premise here is to identify who the key people are and then their direct reports (up and down the hierarchy), firstly as a route for research and intelligence gathering and then to directly influence the key stakeholders. There is often an element of **first mover advantage** when it comes to winning business, so taking the time to map out the organization in as much detail as possible allows you to be able to move quickly when you detect an opportunity. This is especially true if it's time sensitive. Even if you don't know the person, knowing the route to them and leveraging existing internal relationships to get there (ideally the person making the introduction also giving you their support) shows you are a credible partner, and someone they'll hopefully be open to collaborate with. Also, account-based marketing can help with communications with multiple stakeholders in a key account.

In his 2010 book, *Shift*, Craig Elias discusses 'trigger events' and how you can win 74 per cent of the time if you are the first to engage with the key decision maker with the right solution.[24] These can include things like new regulations, changes to market conditions or new entrants. Things that, when they happen, can significantly affect your business. These events mean that the client is compelled to react, and if you have a solution and a pathway to the decision maker, this can lead to winning three out of four proposals. You should try to explore such scenarios in your key account plan, and use them as opportunities to demonstrate thought leadership.

As we are all acutely aware, people are moving all the time, both internally and externally. Consequently, **tracking movements** and changes is also very important, and each move can be both an opportunity and a risk. Such changes can be found out directly from the client through the course of your regular conversations. If it is truly a strategic relationship the client will notify the supplier of key changes. In terms of wider dissemination of information, LinkedIn will capture updates but only when people manually change their own profile. These will be seen on their personal profile and if you have Sales Navigator you can track groups of individual leads and role changes and movements. When you have existing relationships – and especially when they are early stage – **measuring relationship strength** as they blossom is also very important as these are continuously evolving. Examples of this include objectively stating if the strongest one is still the strongest and being able to explain why – this could be in relation to discussing decision makers on a key deal.

Cross-sell and upsell (bringing value to the client organization)

Clients do not like to be sold to, so everything needs to be done in the spirit of creating value for the client organization; they want a partner that understands their business and is supporting them with their growth priorities. The ways to grow their revenue – and yours – will predominantly come from one of two sources, that is either selling something new to the client or selling them more of something they already have. In relation to this, what is called **white space analysis** will help you understand where the opportunities are for growing revenue, and after mapping the key stakeholders (as described in the last section) you will be able to develop a plan to map potential cross-sell and upsell activity. It is called white space analysis as once this exercise is complete you can visualize where revenue is coming from and where it is not. It is where it is not that is considered 'white space'. The output of this effort is a matrix highlighting the following:

- Total revenue from the client.
- Revenue broken down across all of your internal lines of service or products.
- For lines of service with zero revenue that are relevant to your client, define who is the ideal buyer profile or job role.
  - Identify those people and add them to the relationship map if they aren't already included.

- For lines of service with existing revenue, identify any other regions or verticals that could benefit, and then define the ideal buying persona (which will probably be similar to who you are already dealing with).
- Identify those people and add them to the relationship map if they aren't already included.
- The ones with the strongest existing relationship – or with a solid pathway – can be prioritized when it comes to executing growing the revenue.

Doing this properly takes time, and the more complex your product or services offerings, and the larger and more complex the client organization, then the more time consuming the process will be. However, the output of this exercise is a plan that defines how you can grow revenue. The key to co-creating value is your ability to expand your network within the client organization, and this requires **cross-functional collaboration**, whether that is into new business units or into new geographical markets.

At the heart of making this a success is aligning to client priorities (which brings us back to the beginning) and being able to have a conversation with them that demonstrates your knowledge of their business and the challenges and opportunities that lie ahead. As part of this you will express your point of view on how you can help them on this journey. As you get further engrained within the client's ecosystem and are starting to be considered more of a trusted partner than 'just' a supplier, opportunities to co-create or build **customized solutions** materialize. There is a whole array of things that this can mean, from customization of products to personalized support and all the way to creating unique solutions that align with the client's business objectives.

Value being delivered

Any successful engagement is underpinned by value being delivered. This is the metric by which 'success' is gauged, and I wanted to have a short section on this item as it's so important. Establishing what success is, whether that is with a formal set of agreed-upon KPIs or something else that creates a set of tangible outcomes, defining and tracking the success and health of the account is the only way you will be able to monitor progress. And when you have built trust and credibility with the stakeholders, together you can engage in constructive dialogue about performance metrics, progress and areas for improvement. A key part of this is to communicate and reinforce the value you are delivering, for example, by showcasing how the offerings address business priorities, as set out and previously agreed upon.

Business as usual

When it comes to building and maintaining relationships, all of the elements that mattered to the C-suite executives were captured in Chapter 2. Trust is central to this, but there needs to be a sense of a cycle of **continuous improvement,** and the route to that is client feedback. So, seek regular feedback from key stakeholders to identify areas where your organization can improve, and this includes **proactive problem solving.** Such a proactive approach builds credibility and demonstrates your commitment to the client's success. By constantly seeking to improve you will drive client satisfaction, loyalty and trust, and from that comes revenue growth (for both the client and your organization). **Continuously developing relationships** through solidifying existing relationships and making new ones is crucial to sustaining growth, with the focus being on building long-term, mutually beneficial relationships. These help with commercial negotiations and understanding the constant shifting of relationship dynamics at the corporate level.

Going hand in hand with an effective KAM strategy are marketing activities that focus specifically at an account level; this is sometimes referred to as **account-based marketing.** When an account-based marketing strategy is integrated with a well-developed relationship map of the account, it will deliver highly targeted and personalized marketing activities that are aligned with the overall account strategy, Thus aiding engagement, nurturing and relationship building with key stakeholders. Such alignment helps ensure that marketing efforts are finely tuned to resonate with the needs and interests of those targeted.

As discussed at the beginning of this chapter, individual key accounts often generate disproportionate amounts of money for the organization. If you were to ask the much clichéd question 'What keeps you awake at night?' to a global account manager of a key account, in general they'd be much more concerned about losing a key project than winning a key deal. If you are managing a $100 million account and you win a $25 million deal, you may well be up for a promotion, an award and ideally a significant payday. However, if you are managing a $100 million account and suddenly lose a $25 million project (perhaps because you missed something significant), the result of this – in a worst-case scenario – might well be you losing your job. Even if that doesn't happen your reputation will be damaged along with your account losing status. This fear of losing business can lead to almost paranoia about **risks and threats** to the account.

Identifying and mitigating potential risks, such as competitor threats, changing market dynamics, failing projects or shifts in the client business priorities, is of constant concern. The source of data points to support these insights comes from effective research and intelligence gathering. So, the stronger the stakeholder relationships are, the more open and honest communication will be, thereby giving you the best possible insight into the risks and threats to your business.

Summary of examples for mapping existing relationships for key accounts

Onboarding and succession planning

When you have a good understanding of who you have relationships with on an account as well as who on the supplier side holds those relationships, this can become a core part of your onboarding and succession planning activities. When new people join the account, whether they are part of the account management team or part of delivery, the relationship map can be used for them to familiarize themselves. This includes the way the client is structured, who the key people are and who to talk to internally for the right information. On the other hand, if a key person is leaving from the supplier side – perhaps suddenly and unexpectedly – by using the relationship map you are able to act swiftly to identify the relationships they held and transition these to another member of the team. Of note is that this can be done seamlessly and with minimal disruption to the client.

Account health and monitoring

Once you have a view of who the key people are within an account, you are then able to define the engagement strategy. Perhaps it's selecting a set of executives that you will ensure are engaged with on a periodic basis (e.g. monthly or quarterly). As the cycle through the relationship-mapping process is conducted, new relationships will be identified and some key people might have moved out of the client organization. You will also be able to define a strategy around building new relationships in a certain region or business unit, and then monitor the progress over a month or a quarter.

Cross-selling and upselling

The key deals and key projects examples discussed in Chapters 7 and 8 can also be applied here. They are the core methods to grow revenue but, as already discussed, revenue from your **horizontal service lines** is where the growth will come from. So, if you know certain titles are important when positioning a service line targeting, such as the chief revenue officer, CFO or head of digital, then the relationship map can be used to identify and develop those relationships. There is a similar example for **mergers and acquisitions**. When a supplier organization buys another from within the market they usually have an offering that suits a specific job role or department, so the same process can be followed to help identify the right people for this offering by using the relationship map. This could also be a trigger point as each firm will have their own suppliers, so opportunities and threats could emerge in this scenario.

> As already discussed, software is available in the market today that will automatically map all relationships that exist across the organization between a supplier and client or prospect. This makes the visibility into who knows who and execution of all of the examples discussed in Part 3 easier.

There are two case studies in this chapter to illustrate these points. The first is a mini case, based on the experience that awakened me to the importance of relationship mapping. The second is a longer case illustrating a success story of key account development using relationship mapping.

Case study 3: A global bank

This case study is based on past experience and it was this incident that really alerted me to the significance of mapping relationships. Indeed, such was its importance that I feel it was the catalyst for sending me on this 'relationship mapping' journey. This account was a classic case of how to open and grow a key account, starting as a very small project and growing to a £20 million per year account over the course of six or seven years. The supplier was doing very well managing a number of key programmes, the feedback was positive and they were in a good spot. At the time they were one of five suppliers working for this particular client and were the second largest. Then came a conversation with procurement who told them they were going through a supplier consolidation exercise where they would be reducing to three suppliers. This was clearly a serious situation, but although there was some trepidation there was actually some confidence that they'd remove suppliers four and five, so their revenue would be split between the top three suppliers.

Fast forward to the end of the process, which was the typical procurement process of trying to get the lowest rates possible for all the relevant job roles in the various geographical locations. All of that was completed and the supplier was confident as to how that process ended up. However, then came that fateful morning when an email arrived from procurement to say that the process was complete and, unfortunately, they had not been selected as part of this process. Understandably, there was absolute shock and disbelief, with the leader and account team from the supplier side trying to fathom what had happened.

They phoned the CIO, who was the ultimate key stakeholder, explained the situation and informed them that they didn't know what to make of it and were surprised. The CIO responded that they were surprised that they were surprised because it was actually a very easy decision to make. They went on to explain that they had 40 or so people reporting to them and had asked each to name their top three suppliers. They said, 'Do you know how many said you were the number one supplier? Zero. Do you know how many said you were the number two supplier? Zero. And do you know how many said you were the number three supplier? Zero.' Shockingly, that was the end of the discussion but the beginning of the post-mortem.

When an analysis was undertaken to understand where this had gone wrong, it became apparent that all the projects that the supplier was delivering were successful and there were no real causes for concern. The problem, however, was that the people who were being asked for their top three suppliers were not the people this supplier was connected to. When we joined the dots we realized that it was actually their boss who was being asked, and in one case it was the manager of their manager's manager who was being asked. Thus, there was a complete gap in the quality of the relationships from the supplier side at that executive level. Further analysis revealed that around 50 per cent of these executives had only joined in the last two years. So, there was a big gap and no happy ending to that story. The work was transitioned out over the next two years and as these projects stopped, the account was closed.

Case study 4: A global consulting organization

Client: a global consulting organization present in more than 100 countries. While operating as one global brand, it's made up of multiple separate legal entities. These tend to be formed at a country level, but there is also a central function that acts as an overlay structure representing all the countries at a global level.

Supplier: SaaS organization selling enterprise software.

Scope: this case study will straddle the end-to-end process from the initial opening of the account to managing the growth of the key account; that is, from when this client was first engaged with up until the signing of a formal global agreement. The global agreement that was ultimately put into place was the largest deal by total revenue in the organization's history (at the time of writing this book the supplier had been established for more than 10 years).

Timeline: the detail will be explained below under the context section, but the timeline between the first conversations with one of the country-level executives and the global agreement being signed was around eight years and five months. However, if we just consider the timeline from when conversations started with the global executives to an agreement at a global level, then that would be just under three years. But the signing of the global agreement was simply the next level of evolution of the relationship for management of this key account. The delivery of the global project will probably take more than three years.

Relationship capital invested: this section is to highlight the amount of time that was put into this process by the key contact on the client side (who in this case was not the champion but more of a coordinator). This volume of activities was split over two people and the total timeframe of this project was three years and nine months. The key contacts exchanged a little over **1,500 emails** and attended more than **150 meetings** with the supplier. This does not include any of their internal email communication and meetings, nor does it include activities with other people from the client side (other than the key contact). This highlights that we cannot overlook the amount of effort the key contacts need to put in to support such an account.

Context: in this particular case, the corporate structure is such that on the one hand you have the countries that can operate almost as independent entities when making decisions while on the other there is the central function. This central function represents the best interests of the organization overall, promoting best practices and other innovations to drive value at a country level, regionally and globally. So, while there was always the end-game objective to engage with and work with the global management team to forge an agreement for a globally deployed solution, the pathway to get there was part of a careful – and what turned out to be quite protracted – strategy.

Let's start at the point of formal engagement with the central function. This is because it represented the global level, that is when the conversations opened at a global level with the global executives. This required much more strategic thinking and KAM. So, the cycles below will begin there but as part of this context the pathway to get to that point will be explained within this section.

Typically, before the organization would take notice of a software or external solution at a global level it needs to have been tried and tested at a country level. As such, orchestrating that was central to the overarching KAM strategy: sell at a country level, deliver value and then talk to the global level using the internal case study as an example – simple! The time-line between the first conversation with one comparatively large country, which led to a scope for a pilot for that particular country, and the pilot agreement being signed involved a little over four years of conversations. With the start of the pilot came the tangible start of the relationship with that client. At the same time conversations were also happening with two other countries. The pilot converted to an agreement and the other two countries went straight to an agreement without a pilot.

While these deals were going through the sales process (which were all reasonably large deals in their own right) it was felt that it was the right time to execute the strategy for the global agreement. The strategy was two-pronged: how to make money and how to save money. On the make money side, the supplier had the proven success of the first country that had already come onboard and was realizing value, and there were two more countries that had agreed to move forward and were going through the contracting process. So, the credibility and business value had been established at a country level, and it was demonstrated that this value would be exponential when applied at a global level. Thus, the value that would be realized with expansion was solid with a clear path.

On the other side was how to save money, and the strategy was to articulate that if the supplier continued as they were and sold country by country there would be no economies of scale for the client overall. As such, it would cost them a lot more for the same number of licences. So, the business case was built on an example of buying a set of licences centrally versus each country individually buying a smaller set. This was a very compelling argument, and to demonstrate there was future demand the supplier ran a campaign across the organization at a country level to showcase the software and the value, which gathered interest from more than 20 other countries. These conversations were all taking place in the two years prior to (and overlapping a little with) the start of Cycle 1.

Cycle 1 – nine months

The cycles for this case study start as the culmination of a few years' worth of effort is yielding positive results. The focus of this case study is to give an insight into how the relationship-mapping process was implemented and executed so I have avoided giving too many specific details.

Step 1 (mapping of relationships): there was one member organization going through an implementation and rollout and two more going through the final stages of the sales cycle to become a client. So, those relationships were already mapped at a country level. There were also more than 20 other country-level conversations open across the globe, and these were possible because the leadership at country level was mapped for almost 40 of the 100+ countries that the client served. The key part is that the countries all sat under the structure of the global management team. As you can imagine, this account-wide organizational map was large, with the global team at the top and sitting underneath it 40+ country-level maps, some with more detail than others.

Step 2 (research and intelligence gathering): this was a huge undertaking on a key deal and project level and was tackled in a similar vein as the approach in the case studies in Chapters 7 and 8. The main priority was to understand how the global management team operated – that is, what were their priorities and objectives versus those at a country level – and at the same time also researching the identified executives within the additional countries to try to find a lever for engagement.

Step 3 (engagement strategy): from an engagement strategy perspective, at this stage the existing country and the two others that were coming onboard were managed and maintained as separate isolated entities. However, where appropriate there was some crossover; for example, for information security objections from the countries coming onboard the supplier would arrange for them to talk to the existing country that was a client.

The crucial question was how the supplier would engage with the global leadership, and the strategy was two-fold: bottom up and top down. The bottom-up approach involved asking the existing organizations to recommend the solution to their counterparts in the global organization as well as through outreach to the additional countries that were being pursued. The path to generate the 20+ conversations was created through a simple LinkedIn message stating that the supplier already worked with other countries (and also peers in the industry), along with a short note on the value proposition. This created enough interest for a call, during which the value was discussed along with high-level pricing, but it was explained that for the best price an agreement at global level would be best. The supplier asked for this to be passed to the right people on the global side, and through those conversations the same name of who to talk to kept coming up. Subsequently, the supplier did some cold outreach to this person but to no avail.

The top-down strategy was the ace card. One of the senior management team at the supplier had previously worked at this client and although it was many years ago, he worked for someone who was now the chair of the global board. Because these things tend to be a one-shot opportunity, playing this card was something that had been held back until the time was right.

STATUS AFTER CYCLE 1

By now the second of the three countries had come onboard for the supplier and the third was very close to agreeing. As for the global efforts, the outcome of the bottom-up strategy was that in the first few months of Cycle 1 the supplier received an unexpected email from someone at the global level. They wanted to hear more about the solution, which was a big step forward, and these conversations led to deeper discussions and demonstrations to various individuals. Through those conversations there was a much better understanding of global priorities, and the leadership at that level. Of note is that the same key name mentioned previously was coming up again in those conversations. We were told this person was aware of the solution but despite attempts and requests the supplier was yet to meet them directly.

Just after this had happened the ace card was finally played, and a carefully crafted email was sent to the global chair. This resulted in a reply and an introduction to none other than the key person getting mentioned. The first meeting with them and their number two happened towards the end of Cycle 1, and the discussion was very positive. So, all these combined efforts resulted in the opportunity that had been in the planning for a number of years.

Value from the three-step process: the well-executed engagement strategy (Step 3) was fundamental to the progress, both from the bottom-up and top-down perspectives.

Cycle 2 – nine months (total to date being 18 months)

The conversations at a global level were centred on the value proposition of the solution if it was to be expanded globally. This aligned well with supporting the corporate priorities of the global organization as well as providing better value on a per-user level for new countries coming onboard. This in itself would be a major global project, but at the same time something else was happening. For one of the existing countries the supplier's solution was connected to a CRM platform, and together (along with some other technology and process changes) they formed part of a much bigger front office transformation (FOT) for that particular country. This was proving successful, and the plan was to consider this globally too with the supplier's solution becoming part of a much larger and expansive programme. It was previously mentioned that, where possible, the current countries were managed separately from the global strategy; however, because of the FOT programme there was a natural merging of this one particular country and the global effort.

Step 1 (mapping of relationships): in addition to the stakeholder mapping at a country level, the global-level conversations were leading to more stakeholders at that level being identified and mapped. The supplier was also introduced to the global procurement team to start working on the master services agreement, and key people from the CRM provider were identified and mapped.

Step 2 (research and intelligence gathering): the research and intelligence gathering was helping to piece together how the organization was structured and to craft the global value proposition.

Step 3 (engagement strategy): there were now four separate tracks from an engagement perspective: one for each of the countries, who by this time were all onboarded as clients, and the global track. The person in the global level of the organization who first reached out was now the key person helping coordinate everything on the client side. So, they were key to the supplier's success. Of the remaining three countries, two continued to be managed separately, but the third one – for which there was the FOT programme – began to merge with the global-level conversations.

At this point a new key stakeholder was introduced as part of an executive project update meeting, and it was mentioned that they'd be evaluating the technical architecture that had been put in place at a country level and working on how this could be used as a template for a global FOT programme. Running alongside this was the engagement with the CRM provider that would be the main component to the FOT programme, so communication cadence was starting to be put in place.

STATUS AFTER CYCLE 2

Things were starting to solidify for the supplier and positive momentum was building, with the supplier's core value proposition well mapped to the corporate objectives and global priorities. However, about halfway through Cycle 2 there was a shift in the executive sponsorship from the global level of the organization. This involved the retirement of the original key stakeholder while at the same time the person building out the FOT template from the country level to global level was stepping into a leading role. So, there was a shift in ownership to the supplier being part of the expanded FOT programme and aligning to the executives building out that plan. This also led to a change in the point of contact, which transitioned from the global person who had originally reached out to the supplier to a new one who was better aligned to the new stakeholders.

While there had been some cursory and informal commercial discussions, largely anchored on the pricing for the existing members, nothing had been formally shared as the scope wasn't clear. However, from March through to June a lot of work went into building out the value proposition and business value, and there was a huge effort happening on the client side to build up support for the FOT programme.

Value from the three-step process: there will inevitably be personnel changes, especially when you consider the timeframe over which these accounts are managed. So, continuing to cycle through the three-step process on a continuous basis is key. You are refreshing the list of stakeholders, doing the research and intelligence gathering and of course using this insight to plot the right engagement strategy.

Cycle 3 – nine months (total to date being two years and three months)

There was a marked shift in the dynamics of the relationship between Cycle 2 and Cycle 3 to a strategic partnership. There was now a holistic view of the global management team as well as the management layer at the three country levels. In addition, there was the project delivery layer at the three country levels, the relationship with the partner and working together to align a joined-up global solution for the client and – most importantly – there was trust between all parties. This is how a key account should operate. With this shift also came a move to more technical detail including the architecture, information security and data layers, so that was the focus of Cycle 3.

Step 1 (mapping of relationships): there were many more relationships identified and mapped as part of this continuing effort, including with other C-suite officers and their direct reports.

Step 2 (research and intelligence gathering): there was a constant cycle of research and intelligence gathering being conducted to uncover changes at the management level as well as published content at an individual and corporate level. These insights helped to frame the ongoing conversation and also helped to identify new people who the supplier needed to build relationships with.

Step 3 (engagement strategy): fortunately, the new point of contact at a global level was an excellent partner and supported the efforts to get to a level of clarity on how the technical solution would work at that level. This required a lot of meetings at all levels on both sides as well as key meetings with the CRM partner. There was also a regular one-on-one cadence in place between the key stakeholders from the client and the executive sponsor from the supplier.

STATUS AFTER CYCLE 3

The comfort level with the solution and scope was solidifying throughout the early stages of Cycle 3 and the first formal proposal was shared in the middle of the cycle. There were a series of key in-person meetings to discuss and further refine the scope and commercials, with a jointly agreed proposal being settled on towards the end of Cycle 3. This now needed to go to the global board for approval.

Value from the three-step process: the engagement strategy (Step 3) is what held this cycle together, in particular, taking the opportunity to multi-thread when interacting with different people on the client side.

Cycle 4 – 18 months (total to date being three years and nine months)

In the early part of Cycle 4 there were some further personnel changes, with the supplier's executive sponsor leaving and a new top executive brought in. The transition in the relationship with the key stakeholders on the client side was managed successfully, and it remained solid and multi-threaded with high levels of trust between all parties. This again highlights the importance of being multi-threaded. The more integrated relationships there are, the more protected the account is from individual changes in decision makers. During this period there had been ongoing conversations between the legal teams, the master services agreement was signed and the board approval and budgeting process was being worked through.

Step 1 (mapping of relationships): there were some new additions to the global project team that were identified and mapped.

Step 2 (research and intelligence gathering): the same cycle of research and intelligence gathering was done to keep fully informed of changes and other developments.

Step 3 (engagement strategy): in relation to communication there were the usual diarized meetings at a project level (weekly) and executive level (monthly) as well as ad hoc calls when required. As already mentioned, from a key account perspective there were four tracks running: managing the group of three standalone countries and then the global-level agreement that was going through the approval process. The country level was running as 'business as usual' but approval for the global agreement, which would have combined the three countries into the global agreement and rolled the solution out globally, was taking time. During a key in-person meeting the executive sponsor from the client and the top executive from the supplier met, and the outcome from that meeting was a concerted effort to get the agreement signed.

STATUS AFTER CYCLE 4

The global agreement was signed around nine months into Cycle 4. So, it took just under three years from the unexpected outreach from the global team (which came from the outcome of the bottom-up strategy) and the email from the global chairman. This cycle was a more typical key programme status of project planning, implementation, onboarding, training and managing any issues. This is to enable a large global rollout that will likely take three years or more.

Value from the three-step process: when things are 'business-as-usual' it is cycling through the three-step process on a continuous basis, which can be actioned by being habitual about when this is done, perhaps every week or two. But making sure it is done is obviously crucial. Remember that trust needs to be constantly built and reinforced, so going through the cycles will uncover detail and give you points for discussion to have with your client.

What we've learned in this chapter

We have learned the following four key things:

- What key accounts are and why they need relationship maps.
- How relationship maps are used in key account management, using examples of failure and success.
- The significance of the internal champion.

What's coming next

The final chapter is next and explains what you need to do now to put these concepts into action, so you can put down the book and start mapping relationships. Following that it also explains how – once you are conformable with the basic methodology contained in this book – you can take it to the next level by applying some more advanced concepts.

10

What now? Implementing the relationship-mapping process and taking it to the next level

Introduction

DR GRANT VAN ULBRICH, ROYAL CARIBBEAN GROUP – GLOBAL DIRECTOR OF SALES TRANSFORMATION & PERSONAL AND ORGANIZATIONAL CHANGE EXPERT AT SCARED SO WHAT LTD

The very fact that you've made it this far into this book illustrates your determination to set about a change for yourself and possibly others. You are uncovering what is possible and what you could add to your skillset to differentiate your life in new ways. For that, you are to be commended. As you read this chapter you will learn valuable insights into how you will implement this relationship-mapping process. But what you will quickly learn is that when you begin this process, you will experience change as well as causing change to occur for others. How will you manage this change for yourself, your teams and your customers?

Have you ever been taught how to manage personal change for yourself? For most people the answer will be no. Whenever a change scenario occurs, most of us are told 'Don't worry about it, it's going to be ok, you'll do fine'. Or told to 'Just get on with it'. Sound familiar? When they say this to you it rarely makes you feel good. Most people find themselves in fear, worry, stress or anxiety because the body and mind are telling us to do something about the change. However, without a model to use we are left to go into assumption and make decisions without using critical reflection or evidence-based decision making. Often, this can result in us doing nothing and rejecting the change that needs to happen for improvements to be seen.

As a leader, going forward you need to be conscious that your actions create change. We are learning about some very innovative subjects in this book that can dramatically enhance and change our lives. But we need to take the time now to learn how these changes will affect us and others, so we can make the change impactful, manageable and, eventually, successful. This very book is teaching you how to implement a relationship-mapping process. It explains perhaps unfamiliar ways to conduct and implement research, and if you are doing this in a team it will have an impact on others. So, mark my words you are generating change! However, if you want it to work you must think about where you will start and also be mindful of the impact this will have on people you are bringing into the conversation.

Do you want to finish reading this book and do nothing? If you do want to put these ideas into action, then you need a plan to manage you through this personal change. To help you on this journey I would like to introduce you to a new model called SCARED SO WHAT which I researched and created for exactly this type of change event. This involves an app you can download onto your phone that will act as personal coach to help you put these new ideas into practice and reap the rewards that will follow once you take action. SCARED is the reflective part of the model to look at your feelings. It doesn't matter if the change is positive or negative, but obviously in this case it is a positive change that you are willingly embracing.

To begin to manage change, you need to break it down. You do this by asking yourself open questions to each element of SCARED, as follows:

- Am I SURPRISED by this change?
- Am I CONFLICTED or do I CHAMPION this change?
- What ACTIONS can I generate to learn more about this change?
- Am I RECEPTIVE or do I REJECT this change?
- Could I EXPLORE any other options or opportunities?
- What DECISION can I make? Is this favourable or unfavourable? Or am I stuck in indecision?

The SCARED portion of the model is about understanding your feelings so you can make an informed decision and stay away from assumption. Once you've decided – regardless of whether it is favourable or unfavourable – you then are left saying 'So what does this change mean?' or 'So what can I do about it?'. Throughout all of the teachings Dr O'Sullivan has shared, you might be saying that as well. This is where you begin to manage your change strategy by creating your own SO WHAT plan. Continuing onward as your own coach or with others you, ask the following:

- What is my STRATEGY to execute this change?
- Are there any OPTIONS or OPPORTUNITIES I should include?
- Do I have a WAY FORWARD to carry out my plan?
- Do I have HOPE or know HOW I will execute my plan?
- What ACTIONS do I need to take to make my plan happen?
- What do I do to TAKE OWNERSHIP and complete my plan?

Change is constant, and it's personal. How you learn to embrace it turns it into a huge positive opportunity for you. It is my hope that you'll learn the SCARED SO WHAT methodology so that you give yourself every opportunity to make your new learnings a huge success. To learn more or to get the app go to www.scaredsowhat.com. Enjoy your change journey. You have great things in store for your future and this book can help you get there.

Implementing the relationship-mapping process

We've reached the last chapter of the book, and I hope you have found these ideas to be valuable and insightful but now is the time to get up and do something while these messages are fresh in your mind. You may already be doing some of the things discussed, whether it's desktop research about the organization and people you are meeting, checking LinkedIn to uncover unknown relationships or listing and putting key people into an org chart. However, this book is espousing the value of instilling a structure and a process around your key deals, key projects and key accounts, and at the heart of this process are the key stakeholder relationships.

This is something that will be a valuable asset to you and your organization. So, take an objective view of this end-to-end process and use it to build upon whatever you are already doing. This section is broken down into three parts, starting with the impact of AI on the relationship-mapping process. The second part is implementing it at an individual (or team) level, and the third extends on that to implement it more widely across your organization.

The impact of AI on the relationship-mapping process

I've been writing throughout 2023 and as I come towards the end of the book in 2024 it's already clear that 2023 will go down as the inflection point for **generative AI,** which in basic terms is a technology that creates new content by synthesizing existing content. It was the year that ChatGPT exploded onto the scene, and we are now witnessing everything that is flowing downstream from that. So, with the relationship-mapping process I'm trying to balance the way things are done now with the way things will be done in the future. I don't intend to go into a huge amount of detail on what the future may look like, especially considering I'm not an AI expert; however, I will say that the steps outlined in this book will only become easier with AI.

There is often this narrative that AI is 'levelling the playing field' and in some respects that is true, but in this scenario, I think AI is making it easier for those who don't put in the hard work. The ideas in this book take a lot of time and manual effort to implement, and those who are willing to put in that time have seen this have a positive impact upon them and their organization. Because of the manual effort required from various places I suppose some type of AI assistant that would first be directed and can then learn to repeat the process would be a huge step forward. We'll see where AI takes us as part of the next section, and I'll give my quick take based on what I've seen so far.

Implementing the relationship-mapping process at an individual (or team) level

In this section I'll explain the simplest and most straightforward way to get started. It begins with choosing a key deal, key project or key account, and you should choose one that is important to you. At this stage it's not necessary to involve the wider team; you can just take the initiative to get started and as this blossoms you could introduce the idea and share what you have done as part of one of your regular meeting cadences. However, if you are working closely with other team members or have read this book and want to put it into action together, then that is fine too.

You will need access to Microsoft Word, Excel and PowerPoint or the Google or OpenOffice equivalents. As part of each chapter in Part 2 (Chapters 4, 5 and 6) there was detail on what to capture as part of the relationship-mapping process. Now you are ready to put it into action it would makes sense to read Part 2 again.

I have a set of sample templates for tracking the relationships through the three-step process, plus org chart samples, stakeholder profile samples and samples of everything else that has been discussed within this book. I'm happy to share them with you at no cost, so please contact me at www.ryan-osullivan.com. I'd also be happy to connect on LinkedIn, and you can do that by searching for 'Dr Ryan O'Sullivan Introhive' and referencing this book. If for whatever reason you are unable to get the template, open a new spreadsheet and list the stakeholder names in one column and the key headings from Chapters 4, 5 and 6 as the row headings, then populate it with the data as you find it.

With the template in hand it will be a lot easier for you to get started as it covers all three steps, so you can capture all the detail in one place. It's simply a case of going through the relationship-mapping process.

Step 1 involves **identifying the stakeholder relationships** that matter for the key deal, project or account. When doing this for the first time I'd suggest you only choose between five and 10 stakeholders. At this point I recommend going through Chapter 4 alongside the template to refresh your memory of the type of information you need to capture at this stage and why. As you go through the entire relationship-mapping process you will notice that different data points are asked for in different steps. But as you become more familiar with the tracker and where to collect information, e.g. as you identify the LinkedIn URL for Step 1, at the same time you can capture how long they have been in their current role and at the organization. The impact of AI will hopefully render the manual updating of spreadsheets obsolete, and as the AI learns why you are identifying key stakeholders perhaps it could recommend others that will be of interest. This is happening today to some extent with LinkedIn Sales Navigator and will only get better.

For the next part of Step 1 you will also need to **map the stakeholder relationships** which will be started by creating a simple org chart. There are many different types of software available to help you do this, most of which have a free option. Some are mentioned within Chapter 4 and will usually have online video tutorials to explain how they work, but if you have never built such charts before then becoming familiar with how to do this will take time. However, it's probably a good idea to check internally first in case there is one that is preferred within your organization, and it's also worth asking colleagues in case they can recommend one over another. If so, see if they are willing to spend some time to help you, remembering from Chapter 2 that working together on a project, even a mini project like this, is a great way to build relationship capital. As with anything there are pros and cons to each alternative, but one of the trickiest things to master is getting from the list of key stakeholders (e.g. in Excel) to an org chart. Because the list is constantly changing, this process needs to be simple to update in the master Excel spreadsheet and for that data to flow through into the org chart.

You will also likely share this chart with others, so if you are using one that requires a log-in it might cause user experience issues if you share the link and they can't access it immediately. One final thing to be aware of is that when the org chart shifts to a relationship map you will then overlay who from your organization has relationships with who from the client side. Of note is that you will likely include partners in this map as well. This is in addition to the internal 'informal' relationships on the client side as well as other insights such as supporter and detractor notes. So, you will need to learn how to build these perspectives into the relationship map. This is one place where I would hope AI will have an impact, either via an AI assistant or some other mechanism to help with the creation and maintenance of the relationship maps.

Step 2 requires a lot of detective work and most of your time will be spent online trying to find information about the key stakeholders. There are two initial parts to this step, desktop research and intelligence gathering, and it starts with **desktop research**. The template I share offers some structure to this by identifying potential sources of information, with row headings for each of the key social media platforms and other obvious sources. These are all discussed as part of Chapter 5 so go through them with an objective eye to find things that are relevant. And the term 'relevant' can be very broad to include things like them discussing corporate or personal priorities or things that are of interest to them in a personal and/or professional capacity, such as places they are visiting and/or events they are attending. Perhaps there are news articles that reference them or a particular profile of them or their organization.

Pay attention to video content as I find this gives a much richer insight into their personality and communication style, which can be helpful for when you meet them in person. As you find relevant information, copy and paste the link into the template and this way you will be able to keep track of what you find and come back to it later to make sense of it. There is also a column for notes where you can capture your key thoughts based on all the things you are finding. I tend to have one browser page and open different tabs for each of the sources and then rotate through the stakeholders one by one. Sometimes you won't find anything, and this will also tell you something about the person. I've already seen AI impacting this process by enabling you to set up searches on both an organizational and individual level, and the AI automatically capturing and updating this information.

It is possible to connect to sources of choice including their social media sites, and it will learn what is useful and interesting to you and push that forward. It can also learn about your organization's value proposition and top solutions, and then match and recommend timely triggers for you to use.

The second part of Step 2 is the **intelligence gathering**, and this step is your secret weapon. There have been so many times on key deals, key projects and key accounts where I've seen one relationship make the difference between success and failure. I used the analogy of 'panning for gold' in Chapter 5 and that is what it is. But it isn't only finding that one game-changer relationship that happens at this stage; I feel the value of the intelligence-gathering side is often overlooked too. Mapping all the potential sources of intelligence is crucial to help you frame the conversation and narrative when you meet the key stakeholders. And these, perhaps what might be considered lower-level conversations, can lead to many different things at a deal, project or account level as well as in other areas. This insight really makes the difference between having an average (or weak) conversation with a key stakeholder and really impressing them with your preparation. This quote from my doctoral research was already mentioned as part of Chapter 2, but it's powerful enough to repeat for the third time. This was said by a C-suite executive at a global organization:

> What impressed me about him was the diligence with which he researched and talked to a lot of my direct reports, and a lot of other people in the business before he came to me with some ideas about making things better, even before I had thought that perhaps I had a problem. So, here was an individual who I was already beginning to trust and I just felt was somebody who I would listen to.

There is a guide by way of row headings in the tracker I will share to help support this step. As I think about the potential impact of AI, perhaps as it understands the type of connections that are valuable and why, it could not only identify and recommend people within your and your organization's network that could be good sources of information, it could also learn which ones have a high likelihood of helping you. A lot of time goes into this 'panning for gold' process, especially when considering the 2nd-degree connections on LinkedIn, so it's an obvious place for AI to make this more efficient.

The third part of Step 2 is creating the **stakeholder profiles** which are to be used as part of Step 3. When people start actually engaging with stakeholders they'll need something to frame the conversation. These stakeholder profiles are a living document and should be updated as new information is found, but the base content that is used comes from what you find through the desktop research and intelligence-gathering stages of Step 2. That is why I've placed these here in Step 2. But as meetings happen and new insights are found, for example later in this chapter you will learn about personality profiling, this type of information should also be included in the stakeholder profile.

Depending on the importance of the stakeholder and the deal, project or account, you can create a detailed Word document that incorporates all key information from the tracker and offers more space to capture all the key details as well as your notes. A Word document can also be formatted to become something to share with others internally, and I find them easier to manage than trying to populate a PowerPoint slide as there are often formatting issues that take time to fix. However, I've used both options to good effect and sometimes a PowerPoint slide can be easier to include as part of a presentation. The effort required to identify, capture, interpret and format this information into a Word document or a PowerPoint slide is high, so this is also an obvious place for AI to help.

> This point has been made multiple times but how much time you spend on Step 2 and how often you refresh the data is based on how important the deal, project or account is, coupled with how much time you have available. Some ways to industrialize the process are discussed in the next section and AI will certainly help reduce the amount of manual effort required.

Step 3 is the **relationship engagement strategy**. A lot of time and effort has gone into preparing for the moment when you start cutting down the tree, or in this context start building and maintaining the key stakeholder relationships. The stakeholders are identified and mapped and a huge amount of time and effort has gone into desktop research and intelligence gathering. But it's crucial that when it comes time to engage with the stakeholders there is a real, well-thought-out strategy in place as only then will it yield the results you are expecting, and then all the effort will have been worthwhile. If you own the process, consider that you are the maestro of the orchestra or the director of the film, so it's up to you to paint a clear picture and explain the underlying strategy that this relationship-mapping process outlines. Of course, you won't have all the answers but that is what teamwork is all about, so during internal meetings key decisions will be collectively agreed upon. But with regard to implementing Step 3 it will be up to you and the core team to present a plan of action.

> There are two aspects to Part 3 with one being how you are tracking all the detail across the relationship-mapping process, something which can be done in the tracker. The other is how you communicate the strategy to a wider audience, perhaps as part of weekly meetings or some other more formal forum. If senior executives are included, they won't want all the details but will just want a summary and the salient points around what has happened and what is planned to happen. So, bear that in mind as we discuss implementing the process.

Let's imagine this is the start of the first cycle through the relationship-mapping process. While you've done the preparation through completing Steps 1 and 2, the strategy would tend to start with a formal internal meeting. This can either be with the smaller project team or a wider set of people (including your organization's executives) where you would discuss your strategy, who the key stakeholders are and where they fit. To achieve this, **first** the org chart can be used to present the current knowledge. Depending on the context you might want to take a snapshot from whatever org chart builder you are using and put it into a presentation, or you can discuss it directly within the software. You can use this org chart to explain the strategy and pick out the key stakeholders that are important.

Second is a layer deeper which is the plan as to who will engage with who. This detail can be captured in the tracker as per the explanation in Chapter 6. It's the same document that has all the data points and details from Steps 1 and 2, but this is also where you track who from the supplier side is going to reach out to who from the client side. These decisions are made based on all the available knowledge from previous steps, and there will also be a sequence of who you reach out to and when. However, don't make the mistake of reaching out to too many people at the same time. This should be done in a structured and methodical way with adequate time planned to wait for a reply before trying a different route (all discussed and agreed upon as part of the overarching strategy).

If you try to contact too many people at the same time it can create problems and be hard to manage. Remember that each interaction is an opportunity to gather more intelligence, and this will support the next conversation. One person setting up a meeting might be part of a plan for that person to introduce someone else from your team so they can take that relationship forward. While this detail is captured in the tracker you may not be showing that as part of your formal meeting, and it could be a case that the strategy is explained verbally while still referencing the org chart and simply explaining who will do what and when.

This brings us to the **third** item. As you start to assign roles to the people on your team and ask them to build relationships with specific people, they'll want to have some context. For example, if you are asking your CEO to join a meeting with the sponsor and the intended outcome is for them to set up a separate monthly cadence with this executive, then your CEO will want to have more details on this person. This is when you can share the stakeholder profiles that were created in Step 2 and prime them for these interactions. If they are writing content such as an email, you can use information from the profile and draft a template for them to use as a basis for their outreach. This can be done as part of the formal meetings or separate sessions. Thinking back again to the impact of AI, and indeed where it's already at today, it's helping to craft a good email based on inputs that you would be able to share as part of the relationship-mapping process. So, AI could formulate a good foundation for an email that you could add to.

The **fourth** item is capturing and articulating the progress on an ongoing basis. This will be the backbone to your regular diarized meetings where someone (or the group collectively) would explain what has been achieved since the last meeting and discuss and agree upon the plan going forward. As we are walking through the relationship-mapping process here we are assuming this is the first cycle, but as these cycles continue this is where you will see a shift from an org chart to a relationship map. An org chart simply shows where the executives fit within the client organization, but the relationship map will show who from your side (or from a partner) has a relationship with those on the client side. If you so choose it could also depict any internal relationships or conflict on the client side and/or internal alignments that are informally in place. As these are added the relationship map becomes the central discussion document for your regular cadence of meetings.

> If you take a snapshot of the current relationship map for each of your diarized meetings, an interesting pattern occurs if you look back at those snapshots over an extended timeline. As the cycle continues you will see the evolution of your relationships over the course of many months.

We are now in a continuous cycle of rotating through the three steps, from agreeing on a plan in the diarized meeting and executing it, to each individual coming back with insight (or not) and some of them identifying and mapping new key stakeholders, to research and intelligence gathering about those (as well as the existing ones), and then plotting and planning the next round of engagement. I'm not sure if you would find this depressing or invigorating, but it's actually a never-ending cycle, from winning the first deal, to delivering that first project, to that then becoming a key account that you map, and then set about winning more deals and delivering more projects and continuing to expand the account over many years. This relationship-mapping process will provide you with the structure and mechanism to continue this positive momentum.

Industrializing the process: implementing the relationship-mapping process across the wider organization

As individual teams see success when they implement the relationship-mapping process to their own keys deals, key projects and key accounts, others will want to join them on the same journey. And it's perfectly fine for them to follow the same process as outlined in the previous section. However, as this happens within multiple teams there may be more efficient and effective ways for the process to be implemented. This section will discuss how you could industrialize this process as an organization so it better aligns with your own internal systems and processes, and leverages existing investments in technology. It will be discussed under the typical headings of people, process and technology which are often used when explaining business process improvement and organizational development. These three elements are interconnected and should work in unison to achieve successful outcomes.

People: when the individual elements of the relationship-mapping process are considered from a people perspective, a common idea is to assign different parts of the process to different members of the core team. Also, there may well be some internal teams that can support different parts of the relationship-mapping process. For example, perhaps your organization has a separate research team that can help with organizational and individual research, especially for periodic updates to your already defined set of insights.

Training, enablement and change management play a huge role in maximizing the value of any new solution, even if that solution is just integrating a new way of doing something. Training and enablement is available for the core tools forming part of the relationship-mapping process and while there is the assumption that people will know how to use the Microsoft Office suite (or equivalent), LinkedIn and Sales Navigator are being updated all the time, so refreshers are important. However, if you are introducing new software such as a new org chart builder or software such as Introhive, this will require a more concerted change management and adoption effort. You may wish to use this book as part of a training and enablement effort to implement the process more widely within your organization.

Process: as an organization starts to understand the relationship-mapping process and its dependency on the template used to track all the information, they may want to protect this process for a number of reasons. These include information security and data privacy, so they may wish to ensure that no personally identifiable information is captured within the tracker. This would then lead to decisions about where and how to store this data, e.g. deciding that Excel spreadsheets saved locally on individual laptops isn't the best place. So, understanding where the organization wants people to work on deals, projects and accounts will drive a lot of these decisions. For example, storing the org charts as part of the opportunity record within CRM or linking (or copying directly) to account plans within whatever software is used. The same is true for the stakeholder profiles. These are full of very important information, so a process around how they are created and where they are stored needs to be thought through, and then training developed so people are aware.

Technology: understanding which technology stack is being used within an organization is important for a number of reasons, such as for security to ensure that only approved software is being used on corporate systems. For economies of scale and for visibility into corporate spending, knowledge of which people are subscribing to what software is important. This is across all paid-for software from Sales Navigator to org chart software, to relationship-mapping software. In an ideal world these decisions will be made at an organizational level and then the right software will be purchased, the right processes set up, and the right training and enablement rolled out to the end users. However, in reality sometimes new ideas emanate from the field where they are tried and tested to demonstrate that value has been delivered, and then they percolate up and are considered for wider adoption at organizational level.

> This is a complex discussion and one what that requires forethought. Please contact me at www.ryan-osullivan.com for more information about industrializing the relationship-mapping process. I'm happy to share more details including case studies and best practices.

Taking it to the next level

This section will introduce some additional techniques that can be used to go to the next level of detail. These techniques are used by some of the largest and best-funded organizations in the world and in some cases are integrated into the sales and account management processes.

Personality profiling

The importance of personality was highlighted as part of Chapter 2 when a number of the interview participants mentioned it as being a significant factor in whether they thought a relationship was going to work or not. It was primarily from the perspective that, in their experience, when there was a 'clash of personalities' it would have a detrimental effect on the relationship. There are a number of reasons why this can manifest itself and cause issues on the deal, project or account, and at its core is **communication style**. Different personality types have distinct communication styles with some preferring direct and assertive communication where one party takes charge and makes the decisions. Others may respond better to a more collaborative approach based on open discussion and collective decision making. Of note is that the same parallels are true for resolving conflict, with the direct versus indirect approach. So, understanding your key stakeholder's personality will enable you to adapt your communication style to their preferences, enhancing understanding and building rapport and trust.

This extends to the **relationship-building process**. Some stakeholders may appreciate informal conversation and a more personal approach to relationship building while others may prefer to keep the relationship at a professional level and focused on business outcomes. When it comes to their **openness to new ideas** there are also marked differences that can be uncovered by knowing someone's personality. For example, one person may be more open to new ideas and willing to embrace change while another may be more resistant and prefer stability. This will also impact their **decision-making process**. Some individuals may be more analytical and data driven, requiring comprehensive information and evidence before making a decision while others may rely more on intuition or 'gut instinct' and will prioritize emotional factors.

Knowing all of this, it's crucial for suppliers to, first, understand their own personality and, perhaps more importantly, understand the personality of anyone they wish to build a relationship with. With such detail you will be able to use some self-awareness, and try to adapt to avoid irritating or annoying the person on the other side of the table.

There are many different types of personality tests, with some of the most widely known ones being the Myers-Briggs test, the Big Five Personality Test, the DISC assessment and Social Styles. Many of them have online tests that require you to objectively answer questions, and your answers frame your personality style. An internet search on any of these terms will provide a wealth of information, including free online tests. However, such information only becomes valuable when you are able to assess the type of personality of the person you are dealing with and adapt your style to suit them. Personally, I find Social Styles and DISC to be particularly useful for this purpose.

Power maps

The obvious question is what is a power map? This entire book has described the process of identifying, mapping and developing key stakeholder relationships and has discussed the different methods to illustrate the process on a deal, project or account. Central to this, and especially when discussing as a group, is the org chart that has morphed into a relationship map. However, there is an additional dimension – the power map – that can be created which depicts who has the power in the decision-making process, and this is typically used more for key deals rather than projects or accounts.

Imagine an x and a y axis. The y axis represents an individual's influence on the project while the x axis represents their interest in the project. The stakeholders are then populated on the chart using two circles, one smaller

FIGURE 10.1 Example of a power map

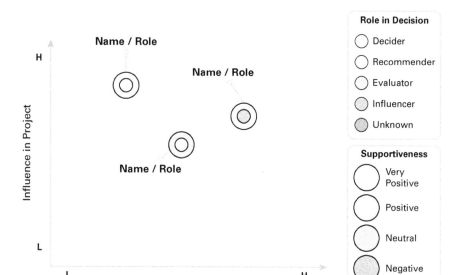

than the other, to denote one of two things. The smaller circle denotes their role in the decision which can be decider, recommender, evaluator, influencer or unknown. The larger circle is a different colour and depicts their supportiveness which can be very supportive, supportive, neutral, negative or unknown. This information already exists from when you populated the stakeholder details within Step 1. An example of a power map is shared in Figure 10.1 (this is in black and white but the actual template is colour coded), and a template included in the tracker I have available for you.

A power map will provide additional insights over and above the relationship map, primarily into the organization's power dynamics. It focuses on who has the authority to make the decision and who has influence over those decision makers. The main goal of a power map is to navigate the power dynamics to achieve the specific outcomes.

Relationship capitalization

Sitting at the heart of relationship capitalization is a proposed solution to the age-old issue of how to value relationships. I first came across this concept in Dr Philip Squire's book *Selling Transformed*,[25] and have been fortunate enough to be involved in a number of presentations where these ideas have been discussed. The premise is simple in that when it comes to an organization's revenue, not all revenue is equal. Think about two organizations with an identical amount of total revenue. As discussed, it's fair to assume that most revenue will come from a small number of key clients (the 80/20 rule).

However, relationship capitalization delves deeper into how we might better understand the quality of that revenue by putting it into different categories, and this could have huge implications for how an organization is valued. Philip has three main categories, the first being the types of contracts that the revenue is captured under such as fixed price contract versus time and material and the contract length. Second, the quality of that revenue, so capturing things such as the profit margin, the number of lines of service the supplier has sold (which will be an indicator of the stickiness of the revenue) and the pipeline of future opportunities. The third element is the relationship capital that exists, and Figure 10.2 illustrates a comparison of two accounts that generate the same revenue but compares them across the details discussed.

Reviewing the contractual details will help build a comprehensive picture of the forward-looking contractual obligations. In this example Client A has a number of existing fixed-term contracts in place stretching a few years into the future while Client B has one short-term contract. While the annual revenue today is the same for both organizations, in the example given Client A is a profitable long-standing client buying multiple service lines for which there is a good pipeline of future projects. In contrast, Client B is new and was only onboarded recently, and the current engagement is the first.

There are three elements of relationship capital. The first is understanding the depth and breadth of the existing relationships, i.e. the structure of the relationship. The second element seeks to understand the quality of the overall outcomes which is determined by the track record of delivering success, and this is the cornerstone of a relationship. It's the key to building and maintaining trust and is measured by client surveys and net promoter scores. The third element determines an alignment of thinking with the client organization, one based around a shared set of values and a good cultural fit, and which can be measured by a survey.

For Client A there are many active relationships across different departments, including at C-suite level. As such, there is alignment with the way each organization works, with a spirit of partnership and comparable cultures. Over the course of the long-standing relationship four successful projects have been delivered, one receiving an industry award and a few others being credited for improving the customer experience of their clients. A joint innovation team is in place with close checks and balances implemented to monitor project success and outcomes, and the client has a sense they are getting value for money.

FIGURE 10.2 Comparing relationship capitalization across two organizations[26]

Metric	Client A	Client B	Source
Contract Types			
Revenue	$10m /year	$10m /year	
Length of relationship	7 years	1 year	Contracts
Contracts	3 Contracts 1) 5 yrs @ £15m TCV 2) 5 yrs @ £20m TCV 3) 3 yrs @ £9m TCV	1 Contract 1) 2 yrs @ £20m TCV	
Finance Contribution			
Profit margin	25%	7%	
Number of vendor 'lines of service' purchased	4/10	1/10	Finance Systems & CRM
Pipeline	$8m	$3m	
Relationship Capital			
Relationship Capital Score	12,784	2,756	
Total number of relationships	50 internal people know 400 at Client A. 20 C-Level relationships	10 internal people know 50 at Client B. 3 C-Level relationships	Introhive
Where do relationships exist	12/15 – 400 relationships within 12 of the 15 client-side business units	4/15 – 50 relationships within 4 of 15 client-side business units	
Quality of service being delivered	4 projects delivered 1 industry award Business value delivered	0 projects delivered 3 formal escalations	CRM Client Survey NPS Survey
Alignment around values & company culture	Joint innovation team	Siloed departments	Consalia Mindset Survey

For Client B, consider that the relationships are concentrated in one area with few at C-suite level, there is some friction developing and there is a clash of culture and values. The single project they are working on is early in its implementation but is already facing issues, and there have been a number of escalations.

If we come back to the original premise regarding how to value an organization, revenue is a key input for the valuation. Then, let's consider that 80 per cent of revenue comes from 20 per cent of the clients. With the current mechanism of interpreting client revenue, the quality of the revenue from Client A and Client B would be considered the same. However, as the example demonstrates, the quality of the revenue is actually very different. Thus, applying the concept of relationship capitalization brings a new dimension to how client revenue is interpreted, providing new ways to value an organization and also providing valuable information for effective KAM.

If the relationship capitalization is officially recognized by the financial community, it would certainly transform the relationship between sales and finance and encourage deeper scrutiny of what constitutes value. How safe is a contract if the client has no trust in the supplier's sales approach? How safe is a contract if there is relationship risk? How predicable are future sales if contract types are short term? It seems safe to suggest that salespeople could justify investments in relationship-building activities if finance teams could see the impact that improving relationship capital would have on their valuation. This would apply equally from a mergers and acquisitions perspective as it would make it easier to quantify the quality of the revenue coming from the acquired organization, and they could conduct a relationship audit as part of their due diligence process.

Concluding comments

As you close the pages of this book and put what you have learnt into action, remember that the journey of mapping key stakeholder relationships is not just about collecting data and making charts and diagrams; it's about unlocking the intricate web of connections that drive success in complex B2B relationships. Every time you uncover an unknown stakeholder, find a new piece of information or gather a crucial piece of intelligence, it holds the potential to transform your business. Embrace the process with curiosity and perseverance, for it is through understanding and nurturing these relationships that growth will flourish. As you navigate your way through your key deals, key projects and key accounts, may this serve as your compass, guiding you towards deeper insights, stronger partnerships and, ultimately, a future defined by collaborative success. So, go forth with confidence, for in the realm of B2B relationships the map you create today is the blueprint for tomorrow's triumphs.

REFERENCES

1   The Nielsen Company (US), LLC, Nielsen Trust in Advertising Sell Sheet, 2021, https://mediamark.co.za/wp-content/uploads/2022/07/2021-Nielsen-Trust-In-Advertising-Sell-Sheet.pdf (archived at https://perma.cc/QRB7-A6H9)

2   C Elias and T Shanto (2010) *Shift*, iUniverse, Bloomington, Indiana

3   H K Gardner and I A Matviak (2022) *Smarter Collaboration: A new approach to breaking down barriers and transforming work*, Harvard Business Review Press, Brighton, Massachusetts

4   R O'Sullivan (2021) Exploring business-to-business relationship quality in the IT services industry, November 2021, https://pure.port.ac.uk/ws/portalfiles/portal/52344477/Ryan_OSullivan_DBA_Minor_Amends_17April22_FINAL.pdf (archived at https://perma.cc/ZBC6-AYGZ)

5   B Hansen, Pasteur's lifelong engagement with the fine arts: uncovering a scientist's passion and personality, *Annals of Science*, 2021, 78 (3), 334–386 (April), p. 382

6   P R Monge and N S Contractor (2003) *Theories of Communication Networks*, Oxford University Press, Oxford

7   W C Moncrief and G W Marshall, The evolution of the seven steps of selling, *Industrial Marketing Management*, 2005, 34 (1), 13–22 (January)

8   T Caponi (2019) *The Transparency Sale*, Ideapress Publishing, Washington DC

9   J L Moreno (2019) *Who Shall Survive?: A new approach to the problem of human interrelations* (Classic Reprint), Forgotten Books, London

10 J Travers and S Milgram, An experimental study of the small world problem, *American Sociological Association*, 1969, 32 (4), 425–43 (December)

11 R E Freeman (1984) *Strategic Management: A stakeholder approach*, Pitman, Boston

12 H Fayol (2013) *General and Industrial Management* (reprint), Martino Publishing, Connecticut

13 F W Taylor (1911) *The Principles of Scientific Management*, HarperCollins, New York

14 M Weber (2012) *Theory of Social and Economic Organization* (reprint), Martino Fine Books, Connecticut

15 M Dixon and T McKenna (2022) *The JOLT Effect: How high performers overcome customer indecision*, Portfolio, Brentford, UK

16 F E Webster, Jr. and Y Wind (1972) *Organizational Buying Behavior*, Prentice-Hall, New Jersey

17   Quote Investigator, To cut down a tree in five minutes spend three minutes sharpening your axe, 2014, https://quoteinvestigator.com/2014/03/29/sharp-axe/ (archived at https://perma.cc/B5ZL-BTWK)

18   Quotefancy, Success is where preparation and opportunity meet, [no date], https://quotefancy.com/quote/1452248/Bobby-Unser-Success-is-where-preparation-and-opportunity-meet (archived at https://perma.cc/5MLQ-XMKK)

19   Gartner, Technology buying behavior: who, why and how, 2022, www.gartner.com/en/industries/high-tech/topics/technology-buying-behavior (archived at https://perma.cc/93ZQ-SJHH)

20   C Senn, The executive growth factor: how Siemens invigorated its customer relationships, *Journal of Business Strategy*, 2006, 27 (1), 27–34 (January)

21   Dr Heidi K. Gardner and Ivan Matviak (2022) *Smarter Collaboration: A new approach to breaking down barriers and transforming work*, Harvard Business Review Press

22   Gardner&Co, Smart collaboration diagnostic, [no date], www.gardnerandco.co/services/tools/ (archived at https://perma.cc/99UK-SHU8)

23   D M McCarthy and R S Winer, The Pareto rule in marketing revisited: Is it 80/20 or 70/20?, *Marketing Letters*, 2019, 30 (2), 139–50 (June)

24   C Elias and T Shanto (2010) *Shift*, iUniverse, Bloomington, Indiana

25   P Squire (2020) *Selling Transformed: Develop the sales values which deliver competitive advantage*, Kogan Page, London

26   Consalia Ltd, Sales Transformation Podcast: Ep. 15 An introduction to relationship capitalisation, with Ryan O'Sullivan, 27 July 2021, www.consalia.com/insights/the-sales-transformation-podcast-ep-15-an-introduction-to-relationship-capitalisation/ (archived at https://perma.cc/5SXH-3B2Q)

INDEX

Page numbers in *italic* denote information within a figure.

Looking for another book?

Explore our award-winning
books from global business
experts in Marketing and Sales

Scan the code to browse

www.koganpage.com/marketing

More from Kogan Page

ISBN: 9781398608511

ISBN: 9781398606807

ISBN: 9781398604766

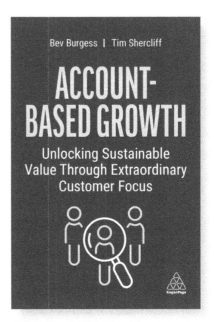

ISBN: 9781398607446

www.koganpage.com

www.ingramcontent.com/pod-product-compliance
Lightning Source LLC
Jackson TN
JSHW050740261224
76012JS00004B/29